The **Obtuse Angler** - Volume 2

A Crappy Cabin
Near a Trout-Filled River

Chris Curtin

ISBN-13: 978-1981656196
ISBN-10: 1981656197
The Obtuse Angler – Volume 2: A Crappy Cabin Near a Trout-Filled River

TABLE OF CONTENTS

FOREWORD

I've never considered myself much of a fly-fisherman, but after 20 years I suppose I have learned a thing or two. Mostly because I invite guys to fish with me that are much better at the sport, and whose tips and techniques I am not above stealing. To be clear, that is not why I fish with Chris Curtin.

As Chris' brother-in-law, my motives for teaching him to fly fish were purely selfish. Mainly, I didn't want to fish by myself while Chris hiked with our wives. Selfishness loves company. Plus I figured if I fell and cracked my head open on a rock, or simply lost my balance and drowned in the river, at least there would be someone who knew approximately where my body could be found.

Somehow I convinced Chris to take up the sport by lending him all of my crappy old gear that I refused to be seen with any longer. Besides he was very hesitant (I don't want to say cheap but...) to buy anything for himself before he was 100 percent committed. And sometimes I think Chris *should* be committed. After the initial sessions of how to do a simple roll cast and how to tie a clinch knot I began to regret my decision to teach him the art of angling. He did however bring extra soda and chips for lunch so that was a bonus.

The reality is Chris has made me look like a very good instructor. Not so much because of my incredible patience with his spasmodic technique but because Chris is an excellent student. He will probably never be known as a great, or even a good fisherman, but his natural curiosity and his perseverance is a big reason, maybe the only reason, why he catches an occasional fish. Chris keeps fishing long after others would have given up - in any given day, week, month or year. As his fly-fishing mentor I am actually learning things from him, such as never wear leaky waders, always bring a rain jacket and don't blow money on crappy equipment that you will only upgrade later - which for the record, Chris does. Did I mention how cheap he is?

Beyond having a reliable partner to fish with, Chris' humor and wit are always good for a laugh. The fact that he laughs at my comments only helps the relationship. I'm always surprised at what Chris notices and remembers from our fishing exploits. I relive them with each story he tells and laugh at things which in the moment didn't seem particularly funny. But his perspective is quite hilarious as it turns out. Even though Chris mostly pokes fun at me and my natural tendency for spontaneous fun, ill-planned adventure and my propensity to lose stuff, I'm still willing to heartily recommend this book. I'm confident you will enjoy his stories as much as I do, as well as his take on what, for me, has been a memorable time on the water with him.

T. Walker

INTRODUCTION

You undoubtedly have noticed that this is Volume Two in the series of Obtuse Angler books. If you are thinking *Oh crap, I didn't read Volume One,* don't panic - it's not necessary in order to enjoy this book. I can catch you up on the action, although if you want to buy Volume One who am I to stop you?

Here's the deal: My wife Kathy and I bought a weekend house a few years ago in mountainous Chaffee County Colorado, near the headwaters of the 1,469 mile-long Arkansas River. It's a scenic two-hour drive from our home in Denver to the cabin, which we make as often as possible. I say "cabin" because it sounds more inviting than what it really is: a manufactured home. Alright, I'm just going to say this: it's a freaking trailer. Although it no longer has wheels, is actually pretty roomy, has an awesome view and a little property, it was still built in a factory somewhere. It was then hauled by truck to Colorado, where it was plopped down onto a piñon-pine studded, but otherwise unattractive lot at 8,000 feet above sea level. We try to ignore the lot and look beyond it to the snow-capped, 14,000 ft. peaks of the Sawatch mountain range.

Never having caught a fish in my 50-year life, I suddenly found myself within easy stroll of one of the best trout streams in the state. My sister Laurie and brother-in-law Todd own a riverside cabin eight miles upstream from our place and eventually Todd convinced me to try fly-fishing. Despite my reluctance to whip around a fake bug with a ridiculously long, impossibly delicate rod while trying to keep my balance on slippery rocks in cold, rushing water, I somehow managed to corral my spastic ineptitude long enough to catch an actual fish! My line-tangling, tree-snagging, bank-tumbling misadventures notwithstanding, I continued pursuing the elusive trout with equipment borrowed from Todd.

Eventually I began to make notes regarding how I caught the few fish I was catching – time of day, river flow, fly patterns – in hopes that it would help me catch more. Before long I realized that information wasn't helping me catch fish

7

as long as I was drifting my flies down the river with all the grace of an ex-con at high tea. So I began to add to my notes all the stupid things I was doing that *kept* me from catching fish. And then I started to add all the dumb things I was doing while hiking, 4-wheeling and exploring around our weekend "cabin" until I realized I had enough ridiculous experiences to make a book.

That first book covered the first four years of my mountainous misadventures. But I didn't stop the shenanigans after four years – as a matter of fact my idiocy has actually increased in frequency. So here you'll read about the next two years – years five and six. This book, like the first one, will never qualify as a "how-to" book. If anything, both of them would fit more neatly into the "how-*not*-to" category. Do as I say, not as I do. Actually if you want to learn anything, *don't* do as I say *or* do. Even though I am fortunate enough to fish at least 30 days per year, I am still very much an uncoordinated boob when it comes to fly fishing. And while I still have my share of misadventures when it comes to hiking and 4-wheeling - and keeping the critters out of the "cabin" has become miserably laughable – more of these Volume Two stories revolve around my continuing efforts to get my act together long enough to catch a trout or two.

Year 5:

SPASTIC INEPTITUDE

Fancy Ass

My fifth year of fly fishing and mountain-cabin owning would prove to be no less challenging than the previous four. Nasty snakes, an invasion of beetles, being chased by a boulder, an encounter with a possible mass-murderer and a fishing road-trip to the stinkiest place on earth would all become part of another typical year. My first "outdoor experience" of the New Year would be a mild affair however, a mid-January Saturday when I went to the Sportsman's Expo in downtown Denver with my brother-in-law Todd and my son-in-law Bronson. (Sounds like an idea for a crappy movie: "The In-laws." (Not to be confused with the hilarious 1979 movie of the same name or the 2003 remake. This one would be more like "Jaws 4: The Revenge" in that it would undoubtedly suck big-time. This is my opinion only. Please don't sue me, Jaws 4 people.) You'll be mildly amused as three middle-aged men try to recapture their youth by purchasing over-priced outdoor gear in a convention hall filled with hundreds of vendors and thousands of sweaty, camo-wearing outdoorsmen. Hey, where did that shark come from?! Aaaah!)

Kathy and I had given Bronson an inexpensive (as these things go) fly rod & reel combo for Christmas because on a few occasions he had expressed an interest in getting into the sport. And now he was anxious to go to the expo to see about getting a deal on wading boots. Todd came because he likes to spend money.

We arrived before they opened the doors, and once they did we made a beeline for the area dedicated to fly-fishing related vendors. Our hope was to check out these merchants before the place got ridiculously crowded, which it almost certainly would on the Saturday before the Sunday Broncos AFC Championship game. We were among the first to run the gauntlet down the aisles, with exhibitors shouting their five-second sales pitch at us as we hustled by. One guy in particular, a guy hawking sunglasses, got on Bronson by saying, "Our sunglasses are twice as good and half the cost of your fancy-ass $200 Oakleys!"

Bronson responded back over his shoulder, "I'm not going to buy anything from you after you insult me." I thought I heard Bronson also mumble something about the guy being an asshole.

Bronson did buy some wading boots, boots that are much nicer than mine. As a matter of fact they cost about three times as much as the rod and reel we bought him. I wound up buying a new but discontinued waist/chest pack, and Todd bought a chest pack as well, although better than the one I bought. I'm starting to feel kind of like a cheapskate.

We then hurried over to a seminar presented by the owner of the fly shop in Chaffee County. The topic was "Spring Fly Fishing on the Arkansas," which was right up our alley. We were able to confirm what we had heard a few days before: 102 miles of the Arkansas River, including the stretch that we fish, had just been designated a Gold Medal trout fishery. Now I really have no excuses not to catch fish.

The day could have ended for us at anytime because daughter Megan, Bronson's wife, was pregnant with their second child and expected to go into labor at anytime. Luckily she waited 36 hours and gave birth to our new grandson on Monday morning, giving us plenty of time to enjoy a greasy, over-priced, almost palatable, convention-center lunch.

Piece of Crap

The time had finally come to fish. After a Friday night, mid-March snowstorm in metro Denver, the weekend forecast for Chaffee County called for sunny and mild days. So after sleeping in a little Saturday morning, Kathy and I wound through Colorado's Front Range mountains to our weekend getaway, pulling in about 12:30. I rigged up, going so far as tying on the flies I was planning to use, while Kathy prepared lunch. (After reading the first Obtuse Angler book, a reader said to me, "Lunch is important to you, isn't it?" My response was that all meals are important to me.) After lunch I drove upstream along the dirt county-road for about two miles to one of my favorite spots on the Arkansas River. I was anxious to get on the water again after a 14-week winter layoff. I was equipped with my new chest pack, two new fly boxes freshly stocked and organized, and a new strike indicator that Todd suggested I try.

Once down at the river I was surprised by the strong flow for this time of year and by the complete lack of ice. The last time I fished here, in late November, the water channel was restricted substantially by ice along both banks. I pulled out Todd's new strike indicator, eager to give it a try after Todd gave me a brief demo on its merits, most notably the fact that it slides easily to adjust, but stays where you want it. This thing is more of a system though, which should have worried me from the start. I'm just asking for trouble using anything that consists of more than one piece.

First you take this little hooked tool and snag your leader with it. Then you flex your leader back away from the tool to make a horseshoe shape, and then slide a little piece of clear tubing off the handle of the tool and over your two parallel pieces of leader. You then grab a hunk of "fine imported wool," position it in the loop you made and slide the little tube up and over the wool to hold it in place. You then trim the wool to your desired size before catching more fish than anyone has caught since the beginning of time. Sounds simple, right? Except if you're me, in which case the tiny tube falls off the leader while you're reaching for the wool, never to be seen again. Then on your second try you are actually smart enough to get your wool ready before doing the tube thing, except when you're trying to get the tube slid up over the wool, your freaking leader snaps in your hand! Which means tying tippet on to your substantially shortened leader, tying the flies back on, stuffing the piece-of-crap strike-indicator system back in your bag and then finally attaching a round, air-bubble indicator, which you should have used from the beginning.

I was fishing fairly deep, having understood that the fish would be down low in the holes this time of year. I also tried to fish water that was getting a good dose of sunshine, so it would be warm enough for insect and fish activity. Before long it was obvious that the small indicator was not buoyant enough to float with the two beadhead flies and a couple of split shot I was using to get the flies down deep. Since I didn't have a larger bubble indicator, I switched to a traditional wool indicator which floated better. Unfortunately this didn't help me catch any fish, so after a while I switched flies. I had the same luck with this set-up, so about an hour later when the sun started to slip behind the mountain and the air cooled quickly, I called it a day.

Brains

I wasn't sure what I did wrong yesterday, but I had no intention of getting skunked two days in a row. So after breakfast and then a few chores, I headed back upriver, hopefully giving the water time to warm up after a 20-degree night. I decided to fish the same basic area as yesterday, which gets good sun on the water, but I parked the truck about a half mile further upstream. As I stepped down off the road bed and into the adjacent ditch I stopped short. Just a few feet in front of me was a dead deer, fairly fresh with its coat still intact. But a couple of things were weird to me. Its entire rib cage and spine had been removed and sat off by itself a few yards away. And the top of its head looked like it had been neatly cut open, with just a hollow cavity inside. Now I'm no expert, but it seems like this area would have been an ideal place for the deer to keep his brains. My guess is that someone removed the top of this deer's head to get his antlers, and then the brain got picked clean by scavenger birds or other critters. I'm still scratching my head over the whole rib cage/spine thing. I'm not a hunter, but I presume it had something to do with field-dressing the deer. Or, perhaps more likely, a space-alien mutilation.

I fished with several different flies for a few hours while freezing my ass off in the cold water before finally coming to my senses and climbing out of the river. I was surprised that I went two straight days without even a strike. In the past this has been par for my course, but I felt like I had been doing enough reading and research over the winter to have a basic understanding of what patterns to fish when and how. I guess the fish hadn't been reading the same books.

Say What!?

Kathy had a social engagement on an early April Saturday to which I wasn't invited, which for some reason is pretty common. It probably has something to do with my reputation as a less-than-interesting conversationalist, which I blame partly on my hearing loss, for which I blame mostly on being in rock bands in my younger days. They were bad rock bands as a rule but they were still loud, and now I spend a lot of time smiling and nodding when I should probably be saying something. Anyway, Kathy wasn't available to go up to the mountains this weekend, so I planned to go by myself and hopefully get some redemption for my fishless weekend of a month earlier. When my brother-in-law Todd learned that I was heading up to Chaffee County, he called to tell me he was going up to his mountain place to work on his kitchen remodeling project and asked if I could haul up some new cabinets and a dishwasher for him. I picked them up Friday night and was rewarded with a 12-pack of stale beer that tasted like it had been wedged in the back of Todd's garage refrigerator since the dawn of mankind.

On Saturday morning I drove up to Todd's place to deliver the dishwasher and cabinets and to fish his private Arkansas River water. It was a cool day and the river was unusually high for this time of year. Apparently the big-snow year caused the water managers to release more water than usual from the upstream reservoirs so they would have more storage capacity available when the big melt began in earnest.

Todd's remodeling work included ripping up an old oak parquet floor with a vibrating machine that was more deafening than the inside of a locomotive engine. Not that I've ever been inside a locomotive engine, but you get the idea. This thing was ridiculously loud and I swear I could feel the thumping vibrations while standing out in the middle of the river. Which brings me to my excuse for not catching any fish: if I could hear and feel this jack-hammering contraption imagine what the fish felt. They must have thought it was the apocalypse the way this thing was blasting sonic mayhem through their normally tranquil world. And what fish can eat at a time like that? The fact that I wasn't catching fish couldn't possibly have anything to do with my fishing skills.

Presently Todd shut the damn thing off, and I ventured up to his deck to sit down and eat my sandwich in peace. But when I was about halfway through he unexpectedly started the machine up again. I tried to finish my lunch, but found it difficult to do with my spleen trying to shake loose from wherever it connects, so I headed back out to the water.

I went upstream a little to try to escape the pounding chaos, but after a while I reeled in my line when I suspected something was amiss with my flies. Amiss doesn't adequately describe what I saw upon investigation. It looked like a fifth-grade science project depicting a tornado made out of fishing line, with my flies, indicator and split shot caught up in it like Midwest trailer homes swirling around inside a real twister. My first temptation was to get busy with the scissors and then start fresh. But I had a new leader on the line that would be lost if I started cutting, so I began the painstaking process of trying to untangle the whole god-awful mess. After ten minutes I was making some real progress when a big, hairy bumblebee landed on, and looked like it was trying to mate with, one of my flies, which I happened to be holding in my hand at the time. Instinctively I swatted at it with my other hand, which at that moment was involved in an intricate detangling maneuver where I had several different sections of line, leader and tippet threaded between my fingers. The good news is that the bee flew off. The bad news is that I lost 10 minutes of work and I was back to my science-fair tornado.

With my new leader once again twisted around like the panties of a big-bottomed woman, I began untangling the whole knotted mess all over again. After another ten minutes I had made enough progress that I was beginning to see some daylight through the crack in the barn door, when a rogue wind blew harshly down the river at yet another delicate moment in my work. The wind swirled my flies around the recently emancipated section of my leader, taking me almost back to square one. *Arggh! Screw it!* I yanked all the crap that was on my line (two flies, strike indicator, split shot) down as far as I could and somehow managed to get it past my tippet knot, where I cut the whole freaking mess out and saved my leader in the process.

I then marched downstream to the other end of Todd's property, trying to get as far away from the bad mojo as possible. I tied on one simple beadhead Prince Nymph and a strike indicator and casted upstream above a large rock. It took me a couple of tries, but I got the fly to drift around to the calm pocket below the rock, where the indicator stalled in the quiet water. Not sure if I had a strike or not, I set the hook and sure enough there was an unmistakable tug. The fish ran downstream and very stubbornly refused to cooperate with my attempts at landing it. It felt like a good-sized fish, but unfortunately I never saw it because, due to my frustrating day, I was too anxious to bring it in quickly and it broke free.

That's it, I've had enough. I reeled in and walked back to Todd's place where mercifully he was done with the deafening, floor-pounding machine. I helped him a little with getting some measurements for his new cabinets and then we made arrangements to head back to Denver. It was only Saturday, but snow was expected that night and we wanted to beat the weather. I decided to leave the truck at our place for the upcoming warm months and ride back to Denver with Todd.

I headed back downstream to my place, but since I had about 45 minutes before Todd would pick me up I stopped at a favorite spot along the river and after three casts got a solid strike. This fish was also quite feisty, so mindful of the fish I had just lost, I worked harder at keeping this one on the line, letting him run a little before bringing him to the net. I was rewarded with my first fish of the year, a healthy, 14-inch brown trout, which I quickly released and sent on his way.

Like a Hurricane

By mid-April Kathy was anxious to spend some time in the mountains since she hadn't been up for six weeks and the weather was getting nice. Todd came up to paint his kitchen and stayed with us again since his place was essentially a disaster zone from the remodel project. On Saturday morning I headed out to fish a few miles north of the house, while

Kathy went for a walk along the river before working on her art, and Todd drove up to his place to paint the kitchen. I can't be certain but I'm guessing that Kathy and I had more fun than Todd.

Once down on the river, at the suggestion of the fly-shop guy, I tied on a big, hairy Pat's Rubber Leg and below that a small nymph. I worked the calm, deep pools along the rivers edge, paying particular attention to the spots that were being warmed by the sun. Within 10 minutes I noticed my indicator stall when it should have been moving. I set the hook and after a bit of a fight netted a 13-inch brown trout that had hit the big upper fly. The fly was really buried in its throat and proved difficult to remove. After working diligently without success, I considered cutting my tippet and releasing the fish with the fly still in its mouth. I didn't really want to leave the big, gnarly fly halfway down its throat though, so for the first time as a fisherman I considered keeping a fish. But as a catch and release guy I didn't really want to do that, anxious to have it return to the water and produce more fish. But it would probably be kind of hard for the fish to get a date with this big-ass fly perpetually sticking out of its gullet, which would probably cause it to go cross-eyed, making a date even less likely. So I kept working on removing the fly, making sure to get the fish back under water frequently. Finally I was able to remove the hook and after some revival it swam off strongly. A few casts later, in another pool just upstream, I caught a rainbow on the small nymph. Wow, this is going to be a good day. I'm not sure I've ever had fish hit both flies I'm fishing. I consider myself quite lucky if they are interested in one.

But I fished for another hour without a strike, so I climbed out of the river and walked back to the truck for my sandwich. As I was eating I noticed I had gotten a text from Todd 20 minutes earlier, saying that he was done with his first coat of paint and did I want to go fish with him at his place. I drove up the dirt county road a few miles while finishing my lunch, pulling up in time to see Todd darting around the yard in his waders, with a scowl on his face. As I got out of the truck he greeted me with, "My leader keeps breaking." I didn't say anything, but I guessed it was from his fancy strike-indicator gizmo that snapped my leader back in March.

I lent Todd a leader and as he came to get it from me he looked at my rig. "You're not going to fish like this are you?" he asked. I explained that I had some success downstream exactly like that. "Your bottom fly is too close to your top fly," he said. I considered the fact that I didn't have any strikes the last hour of fishing, and that Todd probably knew his water better than I did, so I re-rigged for more distance between my flies. But as I was doing so it began to rain and Todd went inside to wait it out, which as it turned out, was the smart move.

I decided that the rain wouldn't amount to much and would probably pass quickly, so I began walking down the road that parallels the river so that I could fish my way back upstream to the house. But within a few steps it began to rain harder, and after a couple-hundred feet it was a certified downpour. By the time I got to the spot where I had intended to start fishing, Mother Nature decided it might be fun to unleash a torrent of marble-sized hail on me. I hastily stepped under a still-leafless tree for protection, which unfortunately, like all the trees in this particular area, was kind of scrawny and offered little shelter, particularly considering the sudden wind that was now whipping the hail around like ice in a blender. For some reason, just at the peak of the storm, while practically humping the tree trunk in an effort to minimize contusions from the projectile ice balls, I decided it would be a good time to take a photo of myself.

This whole time I had been holding on to my fly rod, worried if I set it down the wind would hurl it out of the valley and fling it into outer space. While still holding it I reached into my wader pocket to grab my phone with my other hand, but once retrieved I needed both hands to unzip the plastic sandwich-bag that I keep the phone in for a little protection. But when I reached for it with my rod hand I inadvertently got the rod tip stuck up in the tree branches several feet above my head. And in my effort to free the rod from the tree I actually got it stuck even higher up in the branches. For some reason I was still determined to take a photo, perhaps because without a picture no one would believe the weather I was enduring just to do a little fishing.

I raised the hand that was holding the phone toward the hand that was holding the rod, which by now was stretched up over my head, and with both hands managed to unzip the sandwich bag that was holding the phone. The wind immediately whipped the sandwich bag out of my hand and shot it off toward Kansas, but luckily I maintained a grip on the phone and the fly rod. I tried to position myself so I could photograph the hail-pummeled river in the background - my rod arm still outstretched above my head - then gave my best effort at smiling and attempted to get a photo without exposing the phone to the bombardment of hail. The result was a blurry photo that looked like Ernest Borgnine being pushed out of an airplane and into a hurricane.

Finally the hail slowed and then turned back to a light rain, which gave me the chance to disentangle my rod from the tree branches. I took a few steps to the river and cast in, not really knowing if the storm would be good or bad for fishing. It certainly wasn't good for me because I fished all the way back to Todd's place without a strike.

Deerly Departed

Todd hosts an annual all-star, fly-fishing weekend at his river place every year for some of his buddies that he considers "the world-class, hard-core, fishing elite." I am never invited to join them because basically I am a crappy fisherman. But this year, with his house torn apart from the kitchen remodel, Todd asked if I could host, and I presume actually fish with the big boys. I told him that Kathy and I were planning to go up to our place on his chosen weekend, the first one in May, but that there was plenty of room for him and his pals to join us. It turned out that none of the fishing studs could make it, perhaps because of my growing reputation as a fishing doofus. But that didn't deter Todd, so for our third trip in a row Todd stayed with Kathy and me.

Before departing for the mountain trip on Friday afternoon, Todd asked me via text what he could contribute to the weekend, and I asked him to simply provide the beer of his choice. He had been drinking my beer for the last two trips, and come to think of it, every time he has ever stayed with us. He responded he would get some once we were up in Chaffee County, which made sense. When we arrived on Friday afternoon I asked Todd if he wanted to swing by the liquor store before going to the house. "No, I'll pick up some beer later," he said.

After quickly transferring the weekend stuff from the car to the house, Todd and I headed upstream a couple of miles to fish the river, starting at the tail end of a mile-long stretch of public water. Todd began working the accessible water furthest downstream, so I jumped in a couple of hundred yards above him, both of us moving upstream. After 30 minutes or so of very slow fishing, I moved up into a shallow pool, eyeing the riffle that separated it from the faster water midstream. I casted a few times and then waded upstream around a large rock when I suddenly found myself standing a few feet from a partially submerged deer carcass. This thing looked like it had a broken neck, and there were several bloody areas where some good-sized chunks had been ripped from its flank. I fish this section of river fairly often and I have seen deer carcasses in various states of decay on several occasions - sometimes just a pile of bones. I have also seen scat that, to my untrained eye, looks like it could have originated from a large cat. I'm not saying that a mountain lion roams this area, but I am usually pretty wary here. And I will definitely not be doing any night fishing anywhere near here.

I moved upstream and away from the dead deer, but before long I saw that Todd had come around a bend and into view. I walked downstream a bit, past the deer, and Todd came upstream so we could compare notes on flies and techniques that may be working. Unfortunately fishing was just as slow for Todd as it was for me. Before walking back upstream, I suggested he avoid the pool with the dead deer, and pointed out the location to him. He responded with an uninterested, "OK."

Fifteen minutes later I heard Todd calling, and when I turned around I saw that he was standing in the shallow pool where the deer was, and although I couldn't actually see the deer, which was hidden from my view by large rocks, I thought he must be knee-deep in deer guts.

"What did you say about this area?" he yelled.

"Dead deer!" I responded.

"What?" He couldn't hear me over the rushing water.

"Look down!" I called. Todd looked downstream and then shrugged his shoulders, so I made an exaggerated pointing motion to my feet. Todd finally looked down at his own feet and then jumped back, throwing his arms up and almost flinging his rod into the trees.

"Oh crap!" he shouted. Later, back at the house while we were drinking my beer, Todd told me he was practically standing right on top of the deer.

Spazmaster

On Saturday Todd got permission to fish the river along the private property of one of his neighbors. We drove a few miles upstream from our place, parked the truck and walked across pristine land for about a half mile to the river. We started our day around a bend and just out of sight of the landowner's house, fishing our way upstream all day long without ever leaving their property. Fishing was slow in the morning with a big dry fly and a nymph tied below. I was having a hard time seeing the dry fly in the shady morning light, so I switched it out for a strike indicator. Finally, as the water began to warm toward noon, I got a substantial strike. During the fight the fish jumped through the surface, spraying water that sparkled in the overhead sun, and I could see that I had a large brown trout on the line. But again, being overanxious to bring him to the net after a slow morning, he shook free, leaving me with disappointment and hopefully a lesson learned.

While casting into another lane just upstream I again felt a solid tug on the line. Since I hadn't had time yet to forget about trying to net the last fish too quickly, I played this one a bit, letting him run once or twice before attempting to net him. Once securely in the net, I reached in to remove the hook and was surprised to see an 18-inch rainbow, several inches longer and much heftier than my previous largest trout. After removing the nymph from its upper lip, I decided to snap a quick photo of my prize. While trying to maintain my balance in the swift current, holding the fish-filled net under water with one hand and holding onto my rod with the other, I grabbed my phone with my third hand and took a photo. The picture turned out surprisingly well considering I couldn't see the screen in the bright sun while wearing polarized sunglasses. And I show that photo to anyone who will humor me and take a look at it, although my accomplishment loses some of its luster when I have to explain that the fish is actually bigger than it looks because it is lying in such a huge net.

I bought the new fish-friendly, catch and release net online from a national retailer, anxious to replace the older nylon net of Todd's that I had been using. With that net the fly kept getting snagged on the nylon while it was still in the fishes mouth, unduly complicating my fly removal efforts with every fish caught. But this new net is ridiculously huge, something that wasn't obvious to me when I ordered it online. The first indication that it may be a little large was when it landed with a thud on my doorstep packaged in a refrigerator box. Upon unpacking, it was immediately apparent that I could net a marlin or a sperm whale with this thing, should the opportunity ever present itself. And it looks ridiculous hanging down my back from my neck to my knees, getting snagged on almost every bit of vegetation I walk by.

Shortly after catching that rainbow, which I shall forever hereafter refer to as "Bowzilla," I caught another fish, a good-sized brown that was also quite reluctant to swim into the cavernous giganto-net. After releasing it I continued upstream where I caught up with Todd, who was waiting just downstream from a boulder along the river's edge. Below that huge rock sat a deep pool, fed by a nice seam that skirted along the pool's edge near the center of the river. Todd climbed up on the bank and offered guidance about how to fish this pool, giving me great reminders about coming to a solid stop on my backcast, pausing to let the line load, and then abruptly stopping my forward cast as well. I caught a fish on an early cast into this pool and Todd said he was impressed with how well I recognized the subtle strike. I should have told him that I didn't even know I had a fish on the line, that I was just picking up to recast. But I decided instead to let him be impressed, which of course did not last long.

I had several strikes along the seam that separated the shallow, fast water from the deep calm pool, but had poor technique and timing on setting the hook. Most times I threw the rod tip up so forcefully with excitement that I would fling the fly right back out of the trout's mouth. Other times I was too slow in reacting, attempting to set the hook after the fish had already spit it out. But finally I hooked one, and after a short run I determined it was ready to be netted. But somehow I got my net bungee tangled around my legs, and since I was standing on a slippery rock in the middle of the river with a fish on the line, Todd waded in to help out. He grabbed my net, which snagged my hemostats that were suspended from my chest pack, which in combination with the bungee wrapped around my legs almost caused me to topple into the water. Somehow I kept my balance while Todd netted the fish, but in attempting to bring the fish to the net I lifted my rod up high and got it caught up in an overhanging tree branch. Todd removed the fly and released the fish while I worked to get my rod tip free from the tree, my net bungee still wrapped around my legs, and my hemostats still stuck in the net itself. "Nice job, Spazmaster," Todd said, a backhanded compliment if there ever was one.

A couple of times during the day, I mentioned to Todd that I was getting thirsty, and was anxious to see what kind of beer he would be providing. But once back at the house that evening, he immediately went to the fridge and poured himself yet another beer from my quickly diminishing supply. I was starting to wonder if he had some kind of affliction that made it difficult to enter a liquor store, like beerbuyophopia or something. But when he said he wanted to take Kathy and me to dinner for having him stay at our place for the third time in a month, I decided to stop worrying about the fact that I have never seen Todd provide the beer for any kind of gathering the whole time I have known him, which is now going on 30 years. He is very generous in many other similar respects however, such as providing very good wine. Unfortunately I am not a wine drinker.

We accepted Todd's dinner invitation and suggested a place to eat. But Todd wanted to eat at another spot and since he was paying we agreed with his restaurant choice. But when it came time to pay after the meal, Todd announced that he couldn't find his wallet, sticking us with the tab at a restaurant we didn't really want to go to in the first place. About a week later we received a check in the mail from Todd to pay us back for dinner, but it was only for about half the bill.

On Sunday morning we headed out to fish the river once again along the private property owned by Todd's neighbor. We fished a completely different section of the river, this time downstream of their house. In two days on this property we did not fish any part of the river twice. Once we were on the water Todd announced that he could not find his hemostats. I offered to let him use mine, explaining that I had an old pair I could use, and probably wouldn't need the hemos nearly as often as Todd would to remove flies from fish lips. But Todd is quite attached to his prized hemostats, unhealthily so in my opinion, so he elected to walk the half mile round-trip back to the truck to look for them.

Once again the action was very slow in the morning. After about an hour I sat down on a rock to eat my sandwich and Todd finally reappeared. Not finding his hemostats in the truck, he had driven back to the house to search for them there, but without success. He finally agreed to use my old pair, which I had replaced because they were too crappy even for me. After lunch I changed my fly and within a few casts finally caught a fish. I was surprised that it ate the fly so far out into the current; the other fish that I had caught this year were all in calmer water near the shore.

After another hour or so of fishing our way upstream, we came to a long stretch of river that was constricted in a narrow channel, which made for very swift water that we decided to bypass in search of more fishable water. We climbed up the riverbank and swiftly walked north, peering through the trees with regularity at the river below. After 15 minutes we bushwhacked our way back down the bank to mellower water, where I worked a nice pool for quite a while, convinced that there were fish there. I did get a few strikes here before finally landing a respectable brown.

As I fished my way around a bend in the river, I suddenly saw the house of the landowner whose property we were on. It was a very large log home with commanding views of the prominent snow-capped Collegiate Peaks of the Sawatch mountain range. It was also situated to overlook the river, sitting right above a beautiful pool that Todd was currently standing in the middle of. I guess he was confident that his fishing "pass" included the water that was literally in the shadow of the house.

After all the swift water we had encountered most of the day, that large pool, separated into smaller sections by several lanes of oxygenated water, looked very inviting. I found a nice spot at the lower end of the pool, a little apprehensive about being right in our host's backyard, when Todd came downstream and said, "Here, try this Prince of Darkness. I've caught several fish with it here already." I didn't hesitate to tie the fly on, but I didn't have any immediate success with it so I moved further up into the pool, and even closer to our host's house. I caught a fish almost immediately, then missed a strike or two, and then caught another fish.

I had told Kathy earlier that we would be back to the house by 3:30 for the two-hour drive back to Denver. As tempting as it was to continue fishing now that things were heating up, it was 3:10 and we had a one-mile walk back to the truck. So despite Todd's disappointment, we reluctantly hiked out, our fishing done for the weekend.

Once back in suburbia, Todd fastidiously looked through his car, which he had left in our Denver garage for the weekend, for his missing wallet. Not finding it, he probed *our* car thoroughly, and then came inside and tore our house apart, all to no avail. Once he got back to his house he texted to say that his son Trevor quickly found the wallet in Todd's car, wedged down into the seat cushion. So let's see: for the weekend Todd not only lost his wallet, but also his cherished pair of hemostats. He spent several hours looking for both items, including at least one hour of prime fishing time - and yet he called *me* Spazmaster.

Uncle Fester

Kathy likes to go up to Chaffee County on Memorial Day weekend for the annual Paddlefest, which is a river kayaking competition and celebration in the town of Buena Vista. She likes the energy in the town, the live music and the art-related events put on by the local arts council. Personally, this is one of my least favorite weekends of the year to go to our mountain place because of the holiday traffic on the roads, the crowded restaurants, the high, fast, difficult-to-fish water and the increased kayak and raft traffic on the river. Geez, I sound like a grumpy, old fart. But, so I don't act like an old fart, we usually go to Chaffee County for the annual Memorial Day weekend Paddlefest.

This year I wasn't dreading it too much because we had just bought a new evaporative cooler (a fancy word for swamp cooler dreamed up by some high-priced marketing team) that I was anxious to install before the warm summer-weather hit. We left town on Saturday morning after a rain-soaked Friday night graduation party for our nephew Trevor - Laurie and Todd's son. As it turned out it rained most of the weekend, which I am sure was a bummer for the Paddlefesters, many of whom camp along the river.

Despite the rain, we were able to get the swamp cooler installed on Saturday, which between the weight of the thing and the intermittent showers, took quite a bit longer than we expected. As a result Kathy missed her daytime art deal, and we elected to forgo the soggy nighttime outdoor music. It rained all day Sunday, by which time I had a cold from the waterlogged graduation party of Friday night. Although I felt like crap, we went out for a steak dinner Sunday night just to get out of the house. But to add insult to injury, the restaurant couldn't figure out how to cook a steak medium-well, despite several attempts.

On Monday morning the sun finally came out, so we walked along the river and around the Paddlefest grounds. I felt like I was in the last scene of the movie "Woodstock" where the camera shows a lonely, muddy field littered with trash and the occasional sleeping person, while a few workers dismantled scaffolding and tents. Except this was on a much smaller scale and I didn't see much trash. But I felt bad for Kathy that we worked through, and were rained out of, the weekend festivities. By the time a sunny Monday holiday morning rolled around the party was over. I'm not sure if that was by design, or if everyone had just given in to the rain and gone home.

Bullies, Brookies and Pie

Since Memorial Day had been a disappointment, and since I was still recovering from my cold, we decided to stay home in metro Denver the following weekend. But by Friday evening I was feeling restless from inactivity and called my buddy Tucker to see if he wanted to do some fishing locally on Saturday. Tucker agreed and after some discussion we decided to fish at Beaver Brook Reservoir #3A, a medium-sized lake near the town of Evergreen. Tucker picked me up Saturday morning in his piece-of-crap SUV, a vehicle that always looks like it was very recently on fire, with the flames extinguished just moments ago. We stopped for gas and I asked Tucker how much he would like me to contribute. He hesitated so I offered $5, thinking that would buy about half the gas that our outing would require, but at the same time I spoke Tucker did also, requesting $10. I gave him $10, but anxious to recover some of it I proposed that whoever caught the fewest fish would buy the beer afterwards. Tucker did not respond.

We drove west into the foothills, pulling up to the small parking area 40 minutes later, which triggered my memory of the last time Tucker and I were here. It was about a year and a half earlier, a beautiful fall afternoon that was disrupted by several hours of near-constant rapid gun-fire that almost caused me to lose control of my bladder when I first heard it. I since determined that there is a shooting range nearby - although I'm not sure how legitimate it is - so I was prepared for the gunshots this time.

A ten minute walk brought us to the lake at an elevation of about 8,400 feet. Once there Tucker took off for the far side and I lagged behind, trying my luck here and there with a rubber-legged terrestrial dry fly and a smaller midge tied below that. I was having no luck until I walked across the earthen top of the dam and came to a spot where the shore was lined with large boulders creating some deep pockets. I casted in and immediately hooked a small juvenile trout, not more than five inches long. A few more casts in this area looking for Mama or Daddy resulted in a few more parr, so I moved away, deciding to fish my way back across the rocky base of the dam. It turned out to be a bad move.

The first snake I saw didn't particularly bother me. It was slithering through the rocks, kind of a pale gray/brown/green color with some red marks, only about 16-inches long and about the diameter of my thumb. Kind of a cute little fellow. It quickly slunk from my view among the rocks so I continued traversing the dam, casting as I went. Several yards later I came across a second, larger snake, the same color as the first but thicker and about 22 inches long. *Hmm, that's interesting.* This snake was not so anxious to slink away as the first, so I gave it a wide berth, stepping carefully on the unstable rocks, keeping a wary eye out for a potential reptile ambush here in the middle of this 200-yard long, 90-foot-high rock pile. But the water looked promising so I kept casting into the lake, chastising myself for worrying about a couple of small, probably harmless snakes. And that's when I saw it.

Sprawled out on a rock just a few feet in front of me, motionlessly blocking my path but staring right at me, just daring me to come closer like a middle-school bully, was a thick, four-foot-long snake. This one was about the diameter of my wrist, and yes I have kind of skinny wrists, but still it just had nasty written all over it. It was all I could do not to drop my rod and run away screaming, but thinking back to middle school I decided to deal with the situation. This time I did not throw the first punch, knocking off the snakes glasses and kicking the shit out of it because I was just plain pissed at being bullied. Instead I cautiously back-tracked a few steps, hiked up the dam several yards, and walked a wide circle around Anthony Larabee. Err, I mean the snake. At this point I decided maybe it wasn't such a good idea to fish my way across the dam so I made haste for the far side, concentrating on each step, anxious not to step on or near any of Anthony's friends, which to my mind were lying in wait under each rock, just like in middle school.

Fortunately I made it safely across the rocky dam without additional snake encounters. Subsequent research convinced me that these were Northern Water Snakes, which are said to defend themselves vigorously when provoked by biting repeatedly. Their saliva contains an anticoagulant to keep you bleeding, and if you don't bleed-out, but for some reason are still hanging around, they let go with a foul-smelling musk and start blasting excrement. That sounds like a date I had once, but being the chivalrous guy I am I will not divulge those details.

I decided to switch out my flies, anxious to change my luck from dinky-ass fish and monster snakes to bigger fish and no snakes. There were no fish rising to my dry, or to any natural insect that I could see, so I removed the terrestrial as well as the midge, replacing them with a strike indicator and a small Flashback Pheasant Tail. After a few casts I came across a deep spot along the shore that was protected by the roots of a lakeside tree. I casted beyond here just a bit, giving my fly time to sink as it drifted back toward shore. I saw the indicator dip subtly, so I set the hook and felt a strong tug in return. This time I had hooked something a little more substantial. The fish wasn't too interested in venturing beyond its dark domain, but eventually I coaxed its head above water, where it showed its displeasure with a vigorous jump and a noisy splash, giving me a chance to try and identify the catch. It wasn't particularly large, perhaps 11 inches, but I couldn't tell what kind of fish it was. It was certainly trout-shaped, but the color looked unlike a rainbow or a brown. Once I finally got the rascal in the net it took me a moment to realize what the unique bobcat-pattern, the dark green color and the red, black and white fins meant: my first brook trout. I felt obligated to introduce myself. "Hello Mr. Brookie, it's a pleasure to finally meet you. My name is Chris and I'll be removing your hook today."

I continued my way around the lake, catching a few more small fish, despite the sudden eruption of gunfire from the trees. I had lost track of Tucker by now, so when it started raining I headed back toward the car to see if I could find him and ask if he was ready to leave. I found him where the path around the lake meets the trail to the parking area, sitting on a rock beneath a tree. Tucker gave me his customary greeting, which is a hand held-up to form the letter C. This is his tribute to Baron Von Raschke's signature "claw" move from the cheesy All-Star Wrestling TV show of the 1970's, which for some reason Tucker has been flashing since we were teenagers. I gave him the sign of the claw back before asking, "How'd it go?"

"Yeah, it went just fine, Mr. Curtin." In other words he didn't catch any fish. And for some reason he calls me Mr. Curtin. We've been friends for 40 years - you would think he'd call me by my first name by now. Maybe he's just waiting for me to tell him that he doesn't need to be so formal. On the other hand, he doesn't have any problem calling me Pus Bag or Bung Hole.

When he asked, I told Tucker about my morning. He said, "Well, I'll tell you what, Mr. Curtin, I'll honor our bet by buying you the best piece of pie you've ever had." I had forgotten about my proposed wager, and since Tucker hadn't responded initially, I wasn't sure he had even heard me. "And," he continued, "It's just up the road."

"The best pie I've ever had is around here?" I asked, as sporadic gunfire emanated from the trees once again.

"On Mt. Evans to be more precise."

"What the hell are you talking about?" Knowing Tucker and his constant need for adventure, I was concerned about what he was trying to talk me into.

Last winter, around Christmas time, Tucker and a couple of his equally insane buddies decided they would climb to the top of 14,127 foot Mt. Evans for the purpose of erecting a "Christmas Tree" fashioned from old sailboard masts in the name of art. I probably should mention that Tucker majored in art. It may help explain some of his eccentricities. During the summer months, it is a neat drive to the summit of Mt. Evans, where the views are astounding and the mountain

30

goats and bighorn sheep are abundant. The road closes at Labor Day each year due to the massive amount of snow that accumulates during the winter, not opening again until the following Memorial Day. From the closure gate to the summit it is 14.5 miles and a 40 minute, twisting, turning drive along a very narrow road with sharp drop-offs that threaten to plunge inattentive drivers thousands of feet to a rocky demise. This same 14.5 mile route, with its 3,500 foot elevation gain, can be hiked by someone in excellent health in a mere 5 hours and 45 minutes. One way, on a dry road. This is the route that Tucker and his masochist pals decided to hike round trip, in the dead of winter, with the road closed due to too much snow for the plows.

Did I mention that they decided to add to the challenge by hiking it on the winter solstice - the shortest day of the year with less than 9.5 hours of daylight? Now I'm not a math whiz by any stretch, but I can multiply the one-way trip time by two to come up with an estimated round-trip time. And at 11.5 hours even I can figure out that two hours of hiking would be in darkness, assuming a dry road. But the road would most definitely not be dry. Mt. Evans averages 300 inches of snow per year, 25 feet according to my meager brain. And that's just the snow that's left after most of it blows off. The average wind speed is a ridiculous 28-35 mph, with 123 mph the highest wind speed recorded there. The annual mean temperature? 18 degrees Fahrenheit. That includes the "warm" months too, like July and August.

I tried to talk Tucker out of it. He's in great shape for a 55 year-old, probably better shape than I've been in my whole life. But still I just couldn't see an upside to this. He wouldn't be dissuaded though, so I asked him to at least let me know where they were parking and which vehicle they were taking, which he did. I also asked him to call me when he got down, but on the evening of their climb-day I did not hear from him. I called him but got no response. And then like a mother hen I tossed and turned in bed that night, struggling with the question of *should I call the authorities?* Even though Tucker is currently living alone, he does have family that cares about him, as do his climbing companions, so I reasoned that I was not the person responsible for calling in Search and Rescue.

Tucker finally called me the following night. He said they had begun their climb at 4 a.m. and did not get off the mountain until 10 p.m., 16 hours later, and he had been sleeping ever since getting back to his house. 21 hours later and he still sounded exhausted. He said the snow was deep, the footing was treacherous and the wind was blowing harder than he thought possible, so hard that they were worried they would be blown off the mountain and into oblivion. His hat was blown off, as was one of his gloves, and he had a genuine concern about frostbite to his toes, ears, nose and fingers. He said it was the biggest physical challenge he had ever faced and that he was glad he did it, but he would never do it again. I did not ask him about his sailboard-mast Christmas tree. I assumed he was at least smart enough to leave all that crap behind. I also didn't ask if they reached the summit. Since Tucker didn't mention it I assume they didn't.

So all I could think when Tucker said we were going to Mt. Evans for pie was that during his epic Winter Solstice climb he had somehow hidden a pie among the snow and rocks, just for the sport of retrieving it come summer. It's not as far-fetched as it sounds - this is the kind of stuff Tucker does. "There's pie on Mt. Evans?" I asked suspiciously.

"The best pie you ever had, Mr. Curtin, right there in the gift shop."

I had forgotten about the gift shop and restaurant just below the seasonal closure gate. I agreed to ride up to Mt. Evans with Tucker for pie, but it was more than "just up the road." It took about 40 minutes of driving to get there - 40 minutes in the exact opposite direction of home. No wonder Tucker wanted ten bucks for gas. We sat down in the bar area of the restaurant and ordered our pie, and just to make sure I got my moneys worth I asked for mine ala mode. The pie, by the way, was fine. Tasty, but not spectacular. Certainly not the best pie I ever had.

Excrement Ed

Kathy and I drove up to the mountain place from metro Denver on the first Friday afternoon in June. It was sunny and fairly warm when we arrived, so we took the opportunity to give the swamp cooler we had installed two weeks prior its first test. When we turned it on it was 75 degrees in the den where we installed it. An hour later it had cooled down ten degrees to 65. The bedrooms, being further away from the cooler, didn't cool down quite as fast, but were still considerably more comfortable.

Todd, Laurie and family were also in Chaffee County this weekend, so on Saturday morning I drove up to their place to fish with Todd, while Kathy stayed behind to walk and work on her art. When I got upstream Todd presented me with a new pair of hemostats, which he bought when he purchased a pair for himself to replace those he lost last time out. I figured his gift makes up for about one month of beer mooching out of the 360 months he's been doing it to me. (I mean thank you Todd, I love the hemostats.) The river was running very high and fast from snowmelt, so we decided to try fishing streamers along the banks. But as I was getting rigged up I realized that I had forgotten my wading boots. This was no big deal for fishing the banks at Todd's place, but I didn't want to be limited to standing on the shore all day. So I drove the eight miles back to my place, down the dirt county road that parallels the river, to get the boots.

By the time I got back upstream, Todd decided the streamer fishing wasn't working, so we headed further upstream toward Leadville in search of a lower flow. As we were driving over the bridge where Clear Creek Reservoir flows into the Arkansas River, we noticed that no one was fishing this spot that is usually pretty popular. Zipping along the highway at 60 mph we made a spontaneous decision to pull off at the end of the bridge and give it a try.

As we were gearing up at the truck, Todd discovered that he didn't have his fishing license with him, so I scrambled to unload my gear so Todd could race back in the truck for his license. So far we were getting off to a rocky start. I tied on a rubber-legged attractor dry fly with a small nymph trailing below, but unfortunately I had a hard time seeing the dry in the rolling water. Plus I kept getting snagged on fallen trees in the river, low streamside vegetation and even fairly short natural grass that lined the bank. Waddling around on the grass behind me were two geese with a gosling that I was worried about hooking, although the geese were notably unconcerned, probably because they were accustomed to fishermen whose flies didn't drag the ground on their backcast.

I moved downstream a little where the water was calmer and I could see my fly better, and quickly hooked and landed a ten-inch brown trout. By this time Todd had returned and was fishing much closer to the spillway, still trying the streamer, apparently without success. When I moved downstream even further Todd re-rigged to a dry fly/nymph set-up and worked his way to where I had caught the fish. After a few casts he caught one also, which to me looked like the same fish I had caught, although I suppose it could have been his cousin Stan.

In the afternoon we went further upstream toward Leadville to Crystal Lakes, which, if they weren't' bisected by Highway 24, would sit very scenically in the shadows of Mt. Elbert – the tallest peak in Colorado at 14,440 ft. - and Mt. Massive, just 12 feet lower. I caught two fish relatively quickly, perhaps about 11 inches. Todd caught a very nice-sized trout, about 14 inches, but when he reached for his hemostats - his brand new fancy hemostats - they weren't there. I walked mine over to him, which I had managed not to lose even though I am supposedly the Spazmaster, so he could remove the hook. We were both surprised when the fish slowly started to sink to the bottom upon being released. Todd said it hadn't been an epic battle to land it, and I didn't think it had been out of the water all that long after being netted. Todd scooped his hand down to retrieve the free-falling fish and after a couple of minutes of moving him back and forth underwater the fish swam off, leaving Todd feeling a bit like an emergency-room doctor. He then spent ten minutes searching through his gear for his highly-esteemed hemostats before retreating to the truck, where my old pair was waiting in anticipation of just such an occasion.

After 15 minutes or so of no more strikes, we moved to another area, where Todd struck up a conversation with the next closest fisherman to him, who as it turned out, was quite the talker. This guy, Ed, seemed to be catching fish with regularity, and when Todd asked he said he had been using a

Flashback Pheasant Tail and a red Copper John. Overhearing this I immediately switched from the flies that had gone cold to these two. Straight away I caught a fish on the Copper John, and shortly thereafter a fish hit the Pheasant Tail.

But those flies went cold before long, and when a hard wind started to blow we decided to head back to the truck. As we were gearing down Ed showed up at the parking lot to continue the conversation about whatever he had been talking to Todd about. It turns out he had been telling Todd about a nearby, mystical, secret lake that he said was loaded with brook trout. Although he seemed like a nice guy, we were anxious to end the unnecessarily long conversation, so we asked for directions to the lake so we could go there right this very instant. Ed gave us a long-winded, convoluted explanation on how to find this little-known magical lake, but when Todd and I looked at him with a dumbfounded expression, Ed said, "Just follow me, I'm going that way."

So we followed Ed south down the highway, then southwest down a county road, then straight west down an unmarked, lonely, dirt road. Just as Todd and I began discussing the possibility that, despite his friendly demeanor, perhaps Ed was leading us to his backcountry lair for his monthly murderous rampage, he pulled off to the side of the road in front of us. I anxiously scanned the nearby hillside for any sign of a homicidal accomplice hiding in the bushes before nervously pulling forward. Ed turned off his ignition, got out of his truck and walked toward us. I kept the truck running in case we had to make a quick getaway, or perhaps mow Ed down as he reached for a sawed-off shotgun.

"Well there it is," he said when he got to our truck, pointing to a large mud hole 50 yards down the slope in a brown, treeless meadow. To say it did not live up to our expectations of fishing nirvana would be an understatement.

"What the hell?" I asked, now expecting at the very least a carjacking, or perhaps a violent kidnapping to Ed's nearby renegade survivalist compound where we would be slaves for 20 years. At that point, with his food supply depleted, Ed would undoubtedly chop us up with a machete, boil our carcasses in a 55-gallon drum and put the chunks on a rotisserie over an open fire.

"The lake looks a little dry," Ed said.

"I imagine the fish are too," I replied.

"That's weird," said Todd, "considering all the snow we had this year."

It was weird how dry this entire little valley was. Ed pointed to some other small ponds visible from our vantage point. "There are fish in those ponds. You could try there." These looked even less scenic than our miracle mud hole, surrounded by massive piles of rocks, the byproduct of decades of gold-dredge placer mining in this area. As a matter of fact the whole brown valley was filled with these giant rock piles. Scanning the landscape, I noticed a cluster of decaying wooden buildings sitting forlornly among the rock heaps.

"What's that?" I asked suspiciously, fairly certain it was Massacre Manor, site of Ed's full-moon slaughter-a-thons.

"Ah, those old buildings were moved here from Climax," Ed said with authority.

"I wonder why they would move them here," Todd mused.

Ed didn't know. Subsequent research showed that the buildings were not moved here from anywhere, but instead were built here as headquarters for the mining operations. So basically Ed was full of shit. A nice guy as it turned out, since he didn't try to carjack, disfigure, enslave, rape, or mutilate us, but full of shit. But we didn't know that yet, so when he said we could find other fishable lakes by driving further up the valley toward the surrounding peaks, we bid a hasty farewell and continued up the road. The road that dead-ended at private property just a quarter mile up. A nice guy but full of shit.

We all gathered that evening at Todd and Laurie's riverside place for a mouth-watering grilled steak dinner and a great time visiting with our niece Elise, who had just graduated from an out-of-state college, and nephew Trevor, who had just graduated from high school and would soon be off on his own out-of-state college experience. We all shared stories of our day's adventures, including Kathy who showed us a photo of a watercolor-pencil drawing she had done that day of a rainbow trout. Todd and I told Laurie and Kathy about our fishing exploits and meeting talkative Ed, who may or may not have been a homicidal maniac.

Fences, Antelope and a Ripped New One

Kathy and I drove the eight miles upstream to pick up Todd and Laurie Sunday morning for a return trip to the placer-mining valley of yesterday afternoon. Laurie, me and Kathy were interested in photographing the old buildings against the backdrop of the snow-capped peaks and Todd wanted to try fishing the ponds in the area that actually had some water in them. I put my fishing gear in the truck just in case. We were surprised to find Todd and Laurie waiting out front for us when we pulled up. Usually Todd is either scurrying around trying to find something he can't do without for the day, or lounging in his pajamas over a bacon and egg breakfast.

Soon we were on the highway toward Leadville, then heading west into the valley of the mine structures. (Valley of the Mine Structures – 1952, starring Gregory Peck and Jane Russell. Directed by Howard Hawks. If this isn't a movie (it's not) it should be.) We pulled off the road and parked in a wide pullout about a half mile from the plainly visible buildings in the meadow below. As we sat in the truck contemplating the fence that separated us from the site, two antelope effortlessly ran by, and even though they were moving quite fast, their graceful stride made it seem like they were merely stretching their legs.

We looked but we did not see any no-trespassing signs, and since the wire fence in front of us looked easy to step over, we did just that. Once down near the buildings we came to another fence that surrounded the 3-4 acre site. But this one had a deliberately built, livestock-deterring, gateless opening right at the spot we approached, so we did not hesitate to step within its boundaries.

We were happy to see several weathered wood buildings, mostly still standing and very picturesque, with green hillsides and snow-capped peaks in the background. Todd, still clinging to hope that Ed wasn't completely full of shit, hung around for about two minutes before wandering off to look for some fishable water.

At first the photography looked like it may be challenging as white clouds surrounded the snowy peaks, leaving no contrast between the two and rendering the background featureless. But dark, gray clouds very quickly moved in, while the sun still shone on the peaks and mid-ground trees, making for some nice contrast and rather dramatic photos. We photographed the different buildings from several angles for about an hour and a half until we ran out of ideas. Well, Kathy and I did. It turns out that Laurie only had enough battery power to last about a half-hour, because apparently Todd burned through the overnight battery charge earlier that morning, despite Laurie's warnings, by spending a great deal of time viewing the photos already on the camera.

Todd came strolling back about the time we were finishing up with our photography to report that it was official, Ed was indeed full of shit. As we all walked back to the truck Laurie admonished Todd for discharging her battery just when she needed it. Todd didn't seem too concerned, and come to think of it Laurie didn't act very upset either. Although I suppose she could have ripped him a new one later.

I was curious about the nearby Mt. Elbert Forebay, a good sized reservoir that feeds into the larger Twin Lakes. Once we found it, Todd and I fished from the rocky shoreline while Kathy took more photos and Laurie went for a walk along the lake shore. But after threatening all morning, it finally started to storm within 45 minutes, which sent us scrambling back to the truck and effectively ending today's excursion.

Hypersonic Ladybug

Daughter Megan, her husband Bronson and their kids, four-year-old Haley and five-month-old Kaden, came up to Chaffee County with Kathy and me for Father's Day weekend. Bronson's parents Ben and Lisa drove up from the southern part of the state to meet us there. On Saturday morning Megan decided we should all go to the annual Fibark Festival in downtown Salida, which is the largest town in the county with 5,500 residents. Fibark stands for First In Boating on the ARKansas and is a competition and celebration of all things kayaking. While we don't have anything against it, none of us are particularly into kayaking, so I was a little confused why we would spend a beautiful summer day in such a manner.

Nonetheless the eight of us piled into two cars loaded with all the accoutrements needed to keep a four-year-old and a five-month old alive and relatively tear-free for several hours, drove to Salida, struggled to find a place to park and struggled to find each other after parking in two different locations. We then walked several blocks to the river, which was perhaps the highlight of my day as Haley and I hung back to carefully inspect and poke at anything remotely interesting along the way, such as iron railings, sidewalk worms, detached flower petals and anything more colorful than the last thing.

When we got to the river we found a seat at a picnic table, wondering how we were able to find what appeared to be a prime viewing spot for the on-water activities while so many other people were scattered about, sitting on rocks along the shore. We figured it out a few minutes later when music started blasting at roughly the same decibel level as a jet engine at takeoff from the giant speakers located approximately 1.25 inches behind our heads. But we hung in there long enough to watch three competitors on stand-up paddleboards wobble nervously downriver before they all toppled over 20 feet later when they came to the first bit of turbulence, including one guy who floundered out of control and narrowly missed smashing into a bridge abutment.

After that we walked a block or two over to the park where the festival stuff was going on and found out the real reason Megan wanted to come here: the karaoke contest. Because apparently you can't sing karaoke any night of the week at almost every bar in the state. After she signed up she spent what seemed an eternity buying tickets to the carnival rides so we grandparents could keep Haley entertained while she did her karaoke thing. Apparently after she bought the ride tickets she had to wait for them to be printed in China and shipped across the Pacific Ocean in a leaky rowboat, where a 95-year-old with one leg picked them up at the port in California, then hopped on a unicycle with a flat tire and a missing seat to ride 980 miles, with a two-day layover for some partying in Las Vegas, to deliver them to Megan in Salida, Colorado. All while I sat waiting on a bench in the hot sun without knowing why because nobody bothers telling me what the hell is going on.

Carnival ride tickets finally in hand, the first thing that Haley wanted to do was ride the Ferris wheel. Not the little kiddie Ferris wheel, but the gigantic, rickety, four-story-high Ferris wheel that seemed to be missing half its bolts and was operated by a guy with glazed-over, red eyes who looked like he hadn't slept in three weeks and whose diet probably consisted entirely of Cheetos and Mountain Dew. Kathy, me and Lisa were smart enough to politely decline Haley's invitation to ride with her, but Ben said sure, he would be happy to risk his life to ride the rusty wheel-of-death with her. Fortunately the thing remained upright, at least for the duration of Haley and Ben's ride, and Haley seemed genuinely thrilled with the experience. Ben didn't seem too worse for the wear either.

The next ride was a jet plane which rather mildly went around in circles. Aside from the burning-hot metal seat for which we had to borrow a sweat-stained t-shirt from the operator for her to sit on, this was also a success. The following ride was also a go-around-in-circles thing, this time with a ladybug theme. I think that most juries would agree with my belief that a ladybug-themed carnival ride would be at least as mellow as a jet-airplane ride, if not substantially more so. So we were all shocked, most notably Haley, when the ladybug ride took off with enough force to send it into orbit, and sustained enough speed to keep it there.

As Haley zipped by us in a blur every half second or so, with both hands clenched tightly around the sizzling-hot metal bar, her eyes wide in terror and her lower lip quivering in pre-cry fashion, we tried to reassure her that we were right there and that everything would be OK. I don't think she could see us due to the vision-blurring effects of the g-forces, or hear us thanks to the speed at which she hurtled by.

Eventually I decided my best chance to calm her down was to yell just one word to her each time she whipped by. "It's....OK....Haley...." After what seemed an eternity, the ride operator finally shut the damn thing down and I ran out to pull Haley from the clutches of the hypersonic ladybug. I was very surprised and proud that she did not cry, and when I asked if she was OK she was very brave and said she was fine. I still gave the ride operator my best stink-eye look, although I'm not sure he saw me through his hangover.

Hopefully we made up for the ladybug fiasco by taking her directly to the pony ride, where six or eight little horses in various end-of-life stages limped decrepitly in circles around a center column, stopping frequently for a clean-up detail when one of them relieved itself on the hot asphalt. Luckily the people who were running it were wide awake and cheerful, which leads me to believe they were not associated with the other carnival rides. As a result they were able to cheer up Haley after the great ladybug debacle, so much so that she spent the rest of the day talking about "her" speckled horse, Cappuccino or Cookies-and-Cream or Comatose or whatever it was named.

Consequence of my Spazmosis

I walked the quarter mile from our house down to the river Sunday morning before breakfast and found it running very high and fast due to snow melt. The fly shop guy had suggested trying big dries along the banks, so I fished a Royal Wulff, then hedged my bet by tying a small midge about two feet below that. I fished for an unsuccessful hour before walking hungrily back to the house for breakfast.

Just as we were preparing to leave the mountain house to head back to Denver Sunday afternoon, we learned from Megan that the highway was closed due to an accident. Unfortunately she and Bronson were stuck in the resulting traffic jam with four-year-old Haley and five-month-old Kaden. Also unfortunate was the fact that they had stopped for coffee on the way out of town, and traffic had come to a standstill where the highway traversed South Park, a massive, mostly treeless meadow. Megan's text summed up their experience: *Fantastic. I just peed in a field in front of hundreds of cars.*

Fortunately for me the road closure delayed our departure, so I walked back to the river to try my luck again. I had seen some adult caddis flies along the river, so I tied on a caddis dry, working my way upstream for a quarter mile without so much as an aquatic howdy-do. With the fish showing no interest in dry flies in the cool morning or the warm afternoon, I reeled in to try something sub-surface. As I went to cut off the dry fly I noticed that a very small worm-looking thing (this is probably not the official biological term for whatever it was) had hitched a ride on the hook. So I pulled a similar size and color worm-looking thing out of my fly box, tied it on about two feet below an indicator and got ready for the fireworks. Except the fly was a dud. Or perhaps I was fishing it wrong, which is more likely.

Just before reaching some good-looking water, out of frustration and desperation I replaced the wormy fly with a Mylar-winged Prince Nymph, for no other reason than it looked like the exact opposite of what I had been using. And wouldn't you know that on my second cast I got a solid strike. I saw the flash under water after hooking the fish, and it appeared to be a decent-sized fish. It put up a good fight, so I let it run short distances two or three times before deciding I could net it. I was pleased to see that I had caught a stout 13 or 14-inch brown trout.

My second cast after releasing the fish resulted in another strike. I thought, *wow this is pretty cool, a fish on every other cast.* This one also appeared to be fair sized, and put up even more of a fight than the first. But I had some difficulty getting it in the net, and as I was trying to stretch my rod arm upstream as far as possible and reach downstream as far as I could with my net arm, the fish shook free. I was certainly disappointed, but after two more casts I hooked yet another fish. *So this is what it feels like to catch fish more often than once every four hours.* This brown was kind of skinny at about 11-inches long. As I went to remove the hook I saw that it had barely penetrated its lip, so I said quietly and reassuringly, "It's OK little dude, this will only take a second." That's when I suddenly realized that I say something to all the fish I catch. Usually it's something encouraging or supportive like "you're a good-looking fish," or "we'll have you back swimming around before you know it." Sometimes I apologize if the hook is really buried and I have trouble removing it, "sorry about that buddy." Occasionally I'll say something a little degrading like, "you must not be the smartest fish in the river to let *me* catch you."

By now it was about 5:45 p.m. and we had decided we would head back to Denver at around 6:30, hopefully allowing enough time for the road to reopen. But instead of walking right up the river bank and back to the house, I decided to fish my way back downstream to where I had started, particularly since the downstream fish had yet to see the surprisingly effective Prince Nymph.

After a hundred yards or so I came to a jumble of boulders along the shore that had been difficult to negotiate on my way upstream, so I decided to avoid them by climbing up the bank and going around. But the footing was tricky and the vegetation was thick, so being the klutz that I am, I slipped a few times and got my line, even though secured, tangled up in the bushes more than once. Finally around the boulders, I began to head back down toward the water, but here the footing was even more precarious. As I was approaching a long step down from one rock to the next my foot began to slide and a face plant on the sharp, jagged rocks below looked eminent. As I was falling I truly thought that the consequence of my spazmosis would be one or more broken bones, if I was lucky. I am not proud to say that the phrase I yelled while airborne would be a major barrier to getting into heaven should the need arise in the next few seconds.

But somehow my midair flailing was successful, producing a hard, right-foot-on-a-pointy-rock landing that slowed me down enough before I started tumbling to result in little more than flying gear, several scratches and what felt like a hole in my foot. I expected to come out much worse, particularly considering my ill-advised cursing just when I needed some heavenly intervention. I guess I'll have to work on improving my final words if I'm to have any chance at all with St. Peter.

Just Sit Right Back and You'll Hear a Tale, A Tale of a Fateful Trip

On the first official day of summer Kathy and I drove up into the hills from our Denver home to the Pine Valley Ranch open space park. I had been up here with Tucker a year and a half earlier and I wanted to share it with Kathy, thinking she would enjoy hiking the trails while I fished the river. The North Fork of the South Platte River runs through the park and there is also a small lake, hiking and biking trails and some picnic gazebos.

The day started innocently enough as we walked downstream to the end of the park property where it adjoins a private fly-fishing club. I was hopeful that some of the club's big stockers wouldn't realize that there was a property line and would move upstream to where I would be waiting with my fly rod. Kathy bid me farewell at that point to walk back upstream and explore more of the park. I asked her to give a wide berth to the two stoners we had passed on the way down, who were probably harmless but looked startled and kind of suspicious when we offered them a greeting as they huddled in the trees.

The water was running high and fast from the snowmelt, making wading treacherous. Not familiar with this water I played it safe and stuck close to the shore, which was choked with cast-hindering vegetation. My right, casting arm was on the shore side of the river when facing upstream, so I had to make due with a backhanded flick to get my flies upstream and into the drift. The point I am trying to make here was that I put myself in kind of an awkward situation, which happens more often than not when I'm fishing, and come to think of it, my life in general.

On a very early drift my lower fly got snagged below the water on a submerged log. A few quick wrist snaps failed to dislodge it and since I couldn't wade out to un-snag it in the fast water, I got more aggressive in waving around my rod to free the fly. Not having any luck, I finally gave it a big yank, which resulted in a sickening snapping sound, and the sight of a rod tip dangling from my line. *Crap! ...Wait a second... my tip is still intact.* Somehow I had managed to snag someone else's previously broken rod tip, which had lodged beneath the fly-eating log. *What was that snapping sound?* I looked at my line to see that my tippet broke off at the leader knot, relieved that I had only lost a couple of flies and a few feet of tippet, and not my rod tip. I stuck the broken rod tip in the mud, standing it straight up as a warning to other anglers about the vicious equipment-destroying log dead ahead.

I walked back upstream, anxious to get away from this obviously hexed area, and stopped at a good rock to sit down and tie on new tippet and flies. I fished several spots without any trace of a fish before running into Kathy, who had hiked around some and was now taking photos of the stream and the greenery that surrounded it. I sat down once again to remove the dry fly and replace it with an indicator, and tie on a different nymph. On my first cast afterward I was surprised when the indicator indicated. By this time I was a little jaded from the slow morning and didn't expect a strike, so I reacted slowly and came up empty. I recast into the same spot and was ready this time. The indicator dipped once again, but I set the hook with a little too much gusto, pulling a small fish to the surface and flinging it over my shoulder, where it came free of the fly and arced through the air, landing with a splash 40 feet downriver. As Robert Redford said to Paul Newman in "Butch Cassidy:" "Think you used enough dynamite there, Butch?"

Kathy was sitting on a nearby rock eating lunch, so I went over to join her. As we continued our upriver ramble after lunch, we saw many more people around, groups of people with spin-casting rods searching for a spot to fish along the suddenly-crowded river. It was as if a giant bus had pulled up while we were eating lunch and disgorged a couple hundred fisher-people, all scrambling for a place along the bank. I eventually found a good looking spot that wasn't taken and casted in a time or two. But within a few moments a guy wearing what looked to be a French sailor uniform from a Broadway musical tossed his worm right into where I was fishing. I just looked at the clown, anxious to say something to the effect of, *What the hell, Gilligan? I'm fishing here.* But by now it was obvious that the whole river was filled with fishermen, a far cry from when Tucker and I were here a year and a half ago and had the whole place practically to ourselves. I reeled in my line, climbed up the bank and we walked back to the car to end a frustrating day.

Eek, a mouse!

We arrived in Chaffee County on Friday afternoon in late June looking forward to a weekend of fun, relaxation and maybe a little landscaping work if we were feeling energetic. That dream quickly vanished when Kathy found mouse crap all over the house, most disturbingly on all of the bed pillows. Beds that would be filled with my Mom, sister, brother and their families the following weekend. So we spent Friday afternoon and evening cleaning up mouse poop, looking for and patching holes where the mice could be getting in, laundering the bedding they soiled and buying and setting mouse traps and ultrasonic repellants. Friday night while reading in bed Kathy saw a mouse scurry around the bed and into the closet, so we immediately moved a nearby trap in there. Luckily Kathy is not an "eek, a mouse!" kind of woman. She *is* kind of freaked out by crickets and grasshoppers however.

Upon waking Saturday morning Kathy checked the four mouse traps to discover a solitary casualty. After breakfast I disposed of the unfortunate rodent and then we both went outside to do some yard maintenance, anxious to get outside and away from "The Great Mouse Infestation." After a few hours in the hot sun we came in for lunch and began a more methodical investigation of the premises. What we found was discouraging: mouse crap in every closet of the house. So we pulled everything out of the closets and cleaned them thoroughly, and discarded a few items that were mouse-poop bull's-eyes. I found even more possible points-of-entry, mostly following water and drain lines in the cabinets under the bathroom sinks, and worked to seal those off. After another trip to the hardware store to purchase four more mouse traps for the newly discovered hangouts, we grilled a late dinner of cedar-plank salmon just as the sun was setting behind the Rocky Mountains, which was without a doubt the highlight of the day.

Leotard

Once again Kathy was up before me to check the mouse traps Sunday morning. This time she reported three confirmed kills, which I dutifully removed from the traps and flung across the road by their tails. I cleaned the traps up with the hose, and then farted around for a while to see if I could water two trees from a central sprinkler placement, which it turned out I couldn't. So, a pretty exciting morning.

Around 10:15 I was finally out of the house and on my way to the river. Since I hadn't even seen the river all weekend and didn't really know the conditions, I chose to fish the west bank, where it would be easier to cast forehanded upstream with my right arm. When I got to the river someone was camping at my favorite starting point, so to give us both some elbow room I drove to the next pullout a little further upstream. From here it was a sandy quarter-mile walk to the river through piñon pines and thousands of prickly-pear cacti blooming with vibrant, yellow flowers.

I had some difficulty finding a way down to the river that wasn't too steep, or that actually terminated at the water. The river was still high, running right up to the vegetation, which was thicker here than downstream, or on the east bank for that matter. When I saw the river through an opening in the trees, I headed diagonally down the precipitous bank. But I was surprised at how loose the rocks and soil were here and slipped and slid down the hillside, trying hard not to send rocks tumbling into the river below and spook the fish, while desperately attempting to keep my feet under me.

It made me think of the story a friend and co-worker told me about the time he went camping with another co-worker named Leo. Leo had an old, aluminum-framed camp stool with a canvas seat that he had cut a large hole into for use as a sit-down toilet. While he was using his contraption the canvas seat gave way, sending him butt-first into his just-finished business. But even worse is that for some reason he had positioned the "toilet" directly over a pointy rock, and when he broke through the canvas he landed dead-center on that rock, which of course jammed up into his ass-opening and pretty much ruined his day. Leo thereafter became known as Leo-tard. With this in mind, I was trying pretty hard not to fall on my butt while slipping down the rocky riverbank.

I made it safely down to the shore, found a small opening through the trees and tied on a grasshopper dry fly followed by a Flashback Pheasant Tail nymph. I was having a hard time seeing the hopper in the bright sun, plus it kept getting pulled under by the rather turbulent current. But since I had spent some time tying this rig up I didn't want to abandon it just yet. Fortunately my loyalty was rewarded when I casted along a mellow riffle right near the shore and several seconds into the drift felt a slight tug on the line. I managed to set the hook without having a good view of my dry fly/indicator and pulled in an 11-inch rainbow that had gulped the pheasant tail. A few casts and drifts later a fish rose to my grasshopper. Unfortunately whatever I was watching float down the river wasn't my fly, so when the fish appeared several feet away I saw no reason to set the hook.

Before too long I got the pheasant tail hooked under a submerged log at a spot that I couldn't wade to and retrieve. So I gave my line a desperate, hearty yank and of course lost both flies when my tippet knot broke. But other than losing the flies, it turned out to be a fortuitous break because it forced me to tie on something I could actually see, and was buoyant enough to float well with a trailing nymph. I chose an Elk Hair Caddis with a Copper John below, which turned out to be a good decision. Ah hell, who am I kidding? I just got lucky. Anyway, I could see the Caddis imitation much better than the hopper, and as it drifted downstream after my first cast I watched it stall in the current and immediately lifted the rod tip to hook, bring in, net and release a 12-inch brown trout that took a liking to the Copper John.

Just upstream I saw an area of flat water that was fed by a mellow cascade that to me looked like a great place for fish to feed out of the fast-flowing main channel. I fished this area hard for longer than I should have, bewildered when I came up empty. Directly upstream from here was another shallow pool, perhaps 30 yards long and 25 yards wide. It was divided by two riffles that formed a v-shape and met at the tail of the pool. I moved up to throw in a few flies, but because it was so similar to the non-productive stretch that had just defied me, I already had one eye further upriver.

I was surprised enough when my first cast produced a rise to my Caddis that I wasn't ready for it. I was prepared on my second cast, but when a trout charged up to the surface I could not hook him. Finally, on my third cast, my timing was just right and I nailed a hungry rainbow that crashed up for the big Caddis. I was kind of anxious to bring it in swiftly so he wouldn't spook the rest of the fish here, taking a bit of a chance that he would shake free as I quickly netted it. As I was removing the fly I said to this fish, "It's OK, it's only a flesh wound," before releasing him.

I got several more splashy rises in this pool, and I'm not sure if the fish were refusing my fly at the last second upon closer inspection or if - more likely - my timing was just poor. I had a few fish on the line that got off before I could net them, including one big bastard that basically played dead until I had it inches from the net, when it suddenly and violently shook free. It made me feel like George Foreman in The Rumble in the Jungle, with this fish craftily employing Muhammad Ali's rope-a-dope technique.

I did catch one more fish here, telling this one upon being released, "Thank you, come again," before moving to the head of the pool to have a look at the next stretch. I stood behind a large Volkswagen-sized rock and casted above it along the edge of a riffle that flowed into a deeper pool just on the other side of the rock. It was kind of a tricky cast for me, needing some distance and precision to avoid some big tree limbs that had gotten wedged behind other rocks. But this was my lucky day, because not only did I have the accuracy and distance I needed, but apparently also the right touch to land the fly gently enough on the water to entice a robust strike by what looked to be a good-sized brown. Immediately this fish jumped, flipped, then dove before running downstream into the pool that I just fished and was now standing at the head of. It jumped, flipped and dove again, but I wasn't concerned about spooking the other fish since they were all spooked here already. So I let it run in this pool a little before stripping it in and netting it. The brown was a hefty 15 inches, solid and meaty, and I surprised myself when

I started singing to the fish right in the middle of the river, to the tune of "Poison Ivy:" "You're a big ol' fatty, a big ol' honkin' fatty."

From here I greedily moved up, anxious to catch an even half-dozen fish for the day. After casting my way upstream for a hundred feet or so another fish shot out of the water for what it thought was an easy meal. Luck was with me as I set the hook and successfully landed my sixth fish of the day, a river record for me. Now, I have no doubt that more skilled fishermen would have caught twice that many fish, but I also believe that a year ago I would have been lucky to catch one or two. But today my casting was perhaps the best it's been. I was regularly getting good distance and hitting my spots. I did not get any bad-technique or wind tangles and only got snagged up in a tree once, which I managed to free quickly, allowing my fly to be in the water much longer than usual. After four years of fly fishing I finally felt like I was starting to get the hang of it.

With the Beetles

Kathy and I invited the Curtin family up to the mountain house for the long Independence Day weekend. My mom, my brother Dave, his wife Bronwen and son A.J, as well as Todd and Laurie would celebrate the 4th of July with us. We drove up early Thursday afternoon the 3rd to allow plenty of time for any last minute mouse clean-up that may be necessary. We found two mice in traps and a little bit of mouse poop in a couple of spots. Thankfully it was nothing like the previous weekend when it looked like a mouse-crap bomb had exploded in mid-air over all the beds. But we still had the "bug room" to deal with, previously known as the purple bedroom because of the butt-ugly purple carpet and purple paint. Every summer since buying the place four years ago we have had an infestation of what we now know are carpet beetles. Carpet beetles are very small, harmless insects that apparently feed on, or are otherwise attracted to, organic material such as pet hair and wool (it seems that they were named back when carpet was made from wool). During a bout of frustration last summer we removed the carpet from the bug room since the beetles seemed to be laying eggs in, and hatching from, the carpet. Yeah, we thought it was pretty gross too. We believed this was a major step forward in eradicating them, but that was toward the end of their usual hatch cycle of June thru August, after which they start to go dormant for the season. So we were pretty disappointed when they reappeared this summer with a vengeance.

The previous owner of this house was not a good housekeeper, which we discovered after the closing, and apparently owned a couple of cats. And according to our neighbor, an earlier owner of this house had one or two ferrets that they let roam free inside. And judging from all the dog food that we discovered wedged into every nook and cranny of our laundry room, including inside the motor compartment of the clothes washer, someone owned a dog. I have nothing against cats and ferrets and dogs, unless they are owned by someone who used to live in my house and didn't bother to clean up after them.

Anyway the carpet beetles are back in force and Kathy has been trying to control them with boric acid powder, which they apparently have an aversion to. But with a house full of guests we needed the bug-room for the weekend, so we had to clean up the bugs that had accumulated in the last week and remove all the boric acid, which is not a real good thing to inhale. After cleaning up the room, me and Kathy moved our stuff in there for the weekend, because we didn't want to ask anyone else to cohabitate with potentially hundreds of carpet beetles.

Down by the River

On Friday morning Todd and A.J. played a round of golf, the women went to the July 4 parade followed by an "Art in the Park" affair, and my brother Dave and I walked out the front door of the house, crossed the river and hiked up the hillside to soak in the stunning views of the Collegiate Peaks. In the afternoon the men all fished the river a couple of miles upstream of the house. A.J. and Todd left the truck a few minutes before Dave and I, and once we got down to the river we couldn't find them. I suggested to Dave that his 19-year-

51

old son A.J. was in safe hands with Todd, but Dave said he would be more comfortable knowing where they were. So I recommended that he walk upstream along the abandoned railroad tracks that parallel the river, and I would walk the tracks downstream, and whoever saw them should signal to the other.

After a quarter mile downstream trek while wearing waders in the afternoon heat, climbing down the bank on several occasions to scan the shore, I found Todd and A.J. fishing a nice pool. I whistled, then waved to them, and climbed back up the bank to the train tracks, where Dave was nowhere to be seen. I proceeded to walk back upstream looking for Dave, the whole time expecting him to reappear on the railroad tracks per our arrangement, so I could tell him where his son was, and that he was safe with Todd. I climbed down and back up the loose dirt and rocks that bordered the river channel several times looking for Dave until I finally found him at least a half mile upstream from Todd and A.J., having abandoned the search for his son and fishing without a care in the world.

Dave and A.J. are fairly new to fly fishing so Todd and I were showing them the ropes. A.J. undoubtedly got the better lesson fishing with Todd than Dave did fishing with me. Although Dave was initially having trouble with the concept of stripping in line to remove slack, he did catch a trout on a nymph. I had another six-fish outing, caught on a combination of buckskin nymphs and Elk Hair Caddis dry flies. A.J. caught a fish on a dry fly in tandem with Todd, who had some success of his own. When pushed, Todd reluctantly admitted that he caught 14 fish, most of them in that first pool.

Driving Mocs

Being the host for what turned out to be a fishing weekend with a group that includes my brother Dave and my brother-in-law Todd turned out to be a challenge. Todd is usually in a big hurry to get on the water, while Dave has little sense of urgency in most matters, and none when it comes to fishing. Come Saturday, Dave wanted to scope out Pomeroy

Lakes, eager to fish a high-mountain lake. He said that he, A.J. and Bronwen had taken Bron's new, full-size pick-up partway up the trail earlier in the week while camping nearby, but turned around after a half mile or so, not sure if the truck was too big to negotiate the tight turns of the 4-wheel-drive trail. Todd is not as keen on fishing lakes as the river, but he agreed to go along.

I suggested we stop on the way to buy some leader, tippet and a few flies, all of which I knew we would require a lot of with novice fly fishermen A.J. and Dave. Todd, in an attempt to save some time, tried to convince me that he had enough to go around, although I suspected that as soon as we got to the lake he would bolt for the far side and we wouldn't see him or his kindly-offered tackle again for several hours. When we pulled up to the outdoor shop, A.J. rushed over to Main Street for the annual holiday car show while the rest of us went in and stocked up on fishing stuff. When we were done, in order to give A.J. a little more time at the car show, I went to gas-up the truck. But before leaving I asked Dave to text or call A.J. to let him know we would meet back at the shop in 10 minutes for our trip to the lake. Dave said OK and then began leisurely strolling toward Main Street and the car show, apparently to find A.J. among the hundreds of people and dozens of cars, while Todd bewilderedly watched him wander off.

When I got back ten minutes later Todd was sitting at a picnic table organizing his fly box and Dave and A.J. were nowhere in sight. They showed up in just a few minutes however and Todd jumped quickly into the front seat, ready to get the show on the road. Dave and A.J. spent another five minutes at the back of the truck getting their gear together while Todd drummed his fingers anxiously on the car door.

After a drive down the highway, then a long trek down a county road, then a short climb up a dirt road, we finally turned onto the trail that leads to Pomeroy Lake. It is quite rocky but very scenic as it generally follows a creek for a couple of miles up to the lake, meandering past the old structures that supported the nearby Mary Murphy mine, which sustained the local economy from about 1870-1925. Supposedly the mine was named after a nurse that had cared for one of the claim owners when he was sick. But of course someone, probably Todd, wondered aloud if the story had been sanitized over the years, turning Mary Murphy into a "nurse" from her actual profession of saloon-girl/prostitute. This led to everyone coming up with juvenile, mining-themed double-entendres, the tamest of which was, "after he named the mine after her he gave her the shaft."

As the conversation went further downhill, we continued our uphill trek. Dave asked if he could ride up front for a better view of the trail so he could determine if Bron could bring her truck up here in the future. Todd reluctantly agreed and moved to the back seat, but almost immediately complained that he was light-headed. But Dave didn't fall for Todd's ruse to regain the front seat, instead telling him that due to the elevation, which by now was at least 11,000 feet, some deep breaths and water should help. Todd admitted defeat by taking Dave's advice, followed by a proclamation that he felt better, thank you very much.

After about 1.5 miles of following the rough track we came to a point where the trail got considerably rockier and steeper, the spot where Kathy and I parked the truck and walked the final half mile to the lake on our previous trip here. When I mentioned this, Todd said. "I'm not walking - I didn't bring the right shoes." We all looked at his shoes.

"What the hell are those?" A.J. asked.

"Driving mocs," replied Todd.

We were all so stunned at the absurdity of Todd's footwear that no one could come up with a witty remark.

"Come on Chris, you can drive up this," Todd implored.

Pause. *Sigh.* "Alright, I'll give it a try. But you and your driving mocs are going to have to get out and spot me. And you can explain it to Kathy if a rock punches through the oil pan."

We crept slowly up the path, everyone getting out on several occasions to guide me over the biggest rock obstacles. Walking would have definitely been quicker for anyone not wearing ridiculous shoes. Eventually we made it to the lakes small parking area, where the only other vehicles were three Jeeps modified with lift kits. None of the jeepers said anything other than, "How's it going?" But I could tell they were thinking *Wow, that guy must be a real stud to drive that piece of shit up here. Particularly when one of his passengers is wearing driving mocs.*

As anticipated, Todd quickly geared up and headed for the lake, still at least a quarter mile off over the tundra, and A.J. followed him. After rigging up I helped Dave do the same, thankful that we had stopped for leader and tippet after he pulled an ancient leader out of his pack that had yellowed so much from age that it looked like a three-year-old had taken a highlighter to it. We replaced his leader and then I tied some tippet on, showing him the knot to use, before tying on a dry fly with a trailing nymph.

I walked briskly down to the lake with Dave sauntering behind, eating his lunch as he walked and admiring the jaw-dropping views from our 12,000 foot vantage point. It made me think about the backpacking trips of our younger days and how Dave was usually hiking well ahead of me, head down, legs pumping, anxious to cover more ground before nightfall in search of the ever-elusive, ultimate campsite. I would lag behind, taking in the scenery and the sounds and smells of the forest, just not interested in walking so damn fast. I guess maybe we have both changed. Perhaps Dave is finally willing to slow down and smell the roses after 35 years of demanding-job deadlines. And now that I have a hobby that I enjoy after all these years I'm anxious to make up for lost time.

By the time we got to the lake it was quite cloudy, and we were hopeful that would somehow mean good fishing. We walked around toward the outlet of the lake, where the water flows into the creek that runs back down the steep valley we had just driven up. I had some luck at this spot a couple of years ago and was optimistic it would be equally productive today. Dave and I reviewed the fly-casting technique, modified for lake fishing, before I moved 25 or 30 yards away. I looked over at Dave occasionally to see how he was doing, usually to see him dealing with a tangle, but a couple of times he was just enjoying the picture-book surroundings and eating more food. My brother is not a particularly large man, so I started to feel bad, like maybe I wasn't doing a very good job of keeping him fed this weekend.

I walked over to help him out with his tangles a few times, one of which required some line-cutting and tippet-tying. I asked Dave if he wanted to tie the tippet knot I had showed him at the car, thinking it would help him to learn it. "No," he said bluntly, his hands and mouth full with a snack. So I tied some new tippet on and then Dave said he was having a hard time seeing his dry fly in the water. Since neither of us had seen any fish rising, and Dave said he thought the two fly set-up was contributing to his tangle difficulties, I tied a single nymph to the end of his line and a bright strike indicator further up. Then I suggested he may want to move around a little, and if he wasn't getting any strikes try another spot. I told him I was going to try another area and moved off to do just that.

The area that I picked had a very rocky shoreline. I assumed that since this lake, and therefore these rocks, had been here millions of years, the rocks would have settled in a little by now and provide stable footing. Not so. Almost every step was on a wobbly rock that threatened to springboard me into the deep lake. I kept thinking, *OK, as soon as I get beyond this spot it will be easier walking.* Or, *those rocks look a lot more stable over there.* But it was not to be. After half an hour of probing each rock before I committed to taking a step, I finally got to where I wanted to fish. But on my first cast in the promised land my line-to-leader perfection-loop broke, sending my emancipated leader, tippet and two flies hurtling unrestrained out into the lake. And at the very moment my rig was arcing gracefully and unaccompanied through the air it began to rain. And as soon as my rig hit the water, the wind began to blow.

For a moment there my luck changed, because the wind was blowing right toward me, floating my leader back toward shore. But as I stood in the rain waiting patiently for my leader, tippet and flies to float right up to me the wind suddenly changed direction, and the whole rig started floating away from shore. So I decided to jump out to the closest unstable rock, and then to another a little further out, in an attempt to snag my floating leader with my rod tip. Somehow while balanced on my precarious perch, getting pelted by rain and pushed by the surprisingly strong wind, I managed not to drop my $200 rod into the lake while retrieving eight dollars worth of tackle.

Although by now I was a half mile from the truck, I began walking back toward it so I could get out of the weather to re-tie the perfection loop on my leader. This is a knot I do not yet know by memory, instead having to refer to an app on my phone for a step-by-step how-to video. So I went through the whole painstaking process of again teetering on rock after rock as I made my way around the shore and back toward the truck. Eventually I was back to where Dave was, who hadn't moved from where he had been fishing an hour ago.

"How's it going?" I asked.

"I have a bit of a tangle here."

I looked at his line to see a fist-sized knot of line, leader and tippet. It made me feel a little better about my own fishing skills to know I wasn't the only one who could produce such an immense cluster.

"Based on considerable experience with these things," I said, "I suggest we try to save as much leader as we can and then cut out the tangle."

"OK," Dave agreed.

I slid the tangle down the leader as far as I could and then cut out the remaining knot-ball. Luckily there was enough of the leader left to tie tippet to. I didn't ask Dave if he wanted to tie the tippet knot this time. After I reattached his fly I asked him where the strike indicator was. "I don't know." I attached a new strike indicator and told him he was good to go.

By now it had stopped raining so instead of going all the way back to the truck to tie my perfection loop I found a rock to sit on, pulled out my phone, opened up the video I needed and watched it several times before tying the knot and reattaching my leader to my line. If it weren't for today's technology that allows me to watch a knot-tying video at 12,000 feet and dozens of miles from civilization, I would either still be sitting on that rock trying to tie that knot, or more likely, I would have thrown my rod and reel into the lake and sworn off fishing altogether.

As soon as I got back to the water, a bored-looking Dave moseyed by to tell me that he was walking to the upper lake.

He ambled off and a few minutes later A.J. showed up and threw his fly into the same spot I was fishing. I decided to give him a gentle lesson in etiquette.

"This is a pretty big lake, huh?"

"Yeah," he said.

"Plenty of room for a lot of fishermen."

"Yeah."

"It's nice that there's practically no one here."

"Yeah."

"A lot of room to spread out."

"Oh. Should I fish somewhere else?"

"A little elbow room is always nice."

A.J. walked away and I continued in this area for a time before moving on. At the end of the day, when A.J. and Todd showed up back at the truck together, I realized that I had blown a golden opportunity to spend some quality time with my nephew. And that I had utterly failed as a fishing mentor to young A.J. Screw the etiquette lesson, damn it.

I eventually came to a spot where I could see that fish were rising and I could actually see the insects they were feeding on. As quickly as I could I tied on what I thought best imitated those bugs, tiptoed through the swampy muck as stealthily as possible and made at least 100 casts right on top of the feeding fish. The end result was no fish, no strikes, 100 errors.

By now it was getting late and we still had at least an hour drive to get back to the house, where the women would undoubtedly be perturbed that we had delayed dinner. I saw Todd and A.J. across a relatively narrow finger of the lake, and yelled over that we should get going. They agreed so I headed for the truck. Ten minutes later, as I was approaching the truck, I saw Dave coming down the trail from the upper lake. We reached the truck at the exact same time, after having spent the last couple of hours in the opposite direction. It must be one of those brother things.

Dave told me that the upper lake, which is about a mile away and 500 feet higher in elevation, was still mostly frozen. He said he fished the only opening in the ice he could find, but without success. After another ten minutes Todd and A.J. arrived, talking excitedly about "a bunch of huge cutthroats or cutbows" that they had seen in a small pond they passed while walking back to the truck. I'm not sure why none of us had made this discovery earlier in the day. Surely it would have increased our catch total of one, which Todd had caught on the far side of the lake.

Gearing down at the truck, Todd good naturedly made a big deal out of changing from his wading boots to his "fawn-leather" driving mocs, which he said were exceptionally comfortable because they were "hand-stitched by a virgin native girl on an isolated Pacific island." A.J said it was too bad that the native girl wasn't here so she could help Todd guide us down the rocky mountainside. We did make it down safely, and without any damage to the truck, despite the lack of help from any virgins. And when we got to the house the women were far from annoyed at our tardiness, drinking margaritas as they sat watching the sunset from the deck.

Bent Rod

Two weeks after that July 4th weekend we headed up to the mountains once again. A quick inspection of the house found just one mouse caught in a trap, and a few droppings in the same area. We are making progress, but obviously there is still a problem. So I pulled the clothes dryer away from the wall in the laundry room and plugged up a gap where the dryer vent goes through the floor before it takes a hard right turn and exits the house. While I was at it I reduced the length of the flexible vent-tube that connects to the dryer. I saw no reason for 10 feet of tubing coiled up behind the dryer when two feet would do. I also pulled up the baseboard and carpet tack-strip in the bug room and Kathy liberally reapplied boric acid. Out of curiosity we removed an outlet box cover and found that the box was a very popular spot for the carpet beetles.

Saturday morning promised to be a calm, comfortable blue-sky, mid-summer day, so we drove to little Wright's Lake. In any state but Colorado this would qualify as merely a pond. In Minnesota for instance, it probably wouldn't even show up on the map. But with the exception of large water-storage reservoirs, there are actually very few natural lakes here. So if there is a body of water larger than say a bathtub, it gets labeled a lake. The state leases a few acres here that include not only the "lake" but a section of Chalk Creek that meanders nearby. It's all quite scenic actually, with the Chalk Cliffs (not really chalk, but again this is Colorado) rising imposingly above. There is a ton of fish in this lake, (that's an official unit of measure for fish in a given area: a ton, followed by a boatload and then of course a shitload) but for me they have always been very particular about what they eat. It is not uncommon for three or more fish to swim over and take a look at my fly and then just turn away and swim off. I did catch two fish, but there was a guy on the other side of the lake who had waded out about 20 feet and was catching them with frequent regularity. I imagine it's like shooting fish in a barrel here for good fishermen. We left after about 90 minutes when the sky reneged on its earlier promise and darkened dramatically and rumbled thunder, with wading-guy still standing out in the lake waving around his nine-foot-long lightning rod.

It started to rain about the time we got back to the house and by the time we finished lunch it was raining harder than I have ever seen it rain here. After about an hour it slowed and started to clear, so I prepared to head out to fish the river. By the time I was ready to go the rain had stopped, so I threw the gear in the truck and drove upriver a couple of miles. But as soon as I pulled up it started to rain again, stranding me in the truck for several minutes while waiting for it to slow down. Once it did I put on my rain jacket, geared up and walked down to the river. And of course once there the rain stopped completely and the sun came out and I was saddled with the hot rain-jacket the rest of the afternoon.

I worked my way upriver for two hours without a single strike when finally a fish jumped up for my Elk-Hair Caddis directly upstream from where I was standing in the river. I set the hook and the fish took off, swimming straight at me. Before I knew it the trout swam right between my legs and continued downriver, pulling the line up to my crotch and bending my rod unnaturally. My fly rod that is. So I was standing in the river facing upstream, I had a fish on the line downstream of me, I was straddling the line which was pulled up tight against my crotch and I was trying to keep the rod tip up (still talking fly rod here) and tension on the line so I didn't lose the fish. I couldn't think of anything to do other than try to net the fish, so I began stripping in line like I normally would, thankful that I was wearing waders and not just shorts. But since I was trapped in place I had no choice but to work directly against the current, and it was only a matter of seconds before the fish shook free. I climbed out of the river and called it a day, admitting defeat to the obviously smarter fish.

Once back at the house I fired up the grill and cooked buffalo burgers, and then after dinner Kathy and I walked along the river to the park where a bluegrass band was playing. After an hour or so we strolled back toward the cabin in time to see the river glowing pink, reflecting the last of the day's sunset.

Busted

After breakfast the following morning and a stop at the fly shop, I fished the west shore of the river directly across from where I fished yesterday. I had quite a bit of success here - for me - a few weeks before and was anxious to change my luck of yesterday. I fished four hours, with a Yellow Sally and other yellow or light-colored flies, with only 3-4 tepid strikes and no fish. At one point I felt a weirdness in my line during a cast and reeled in to find a tangled mess. I may be very, very slowly getting better at this fly fishing stuff, and perhaps one of the things I'm happiest about is a reduction in the number and size of my tangles. But now, to actually *feel* a tangle as it happens? That's something I can be proud of. *He may not be much of a fisherman, Jim, but that guy can sure feel a tangle coming on.* What's next, actually avoiding tangles all together? Nah, that will never happen. Feeling a little puffed-up from my new-found skill, I sat on a rock in the river to untangle the mess. Unfortunately as soon as I sat down I slipped right off the rock and landed flat on my ass in the knee-deep water.

First a tangle, and now a splash-down. I can tell when I start to tire, and when I do bad things begin to happen. So after untangling my line, which was more complicated after the dunking, I climbed out of the river, up the bank and hiked back to the truck. As I was gearing down I saw through the piñon trees a Bureau of Land Management ranger driving on the dirt access road. He made a sudden stop, and then pulled off and headed down the trail to where I was parked. After getting out of his truck and exchanging pleasantries, he got down to business.

"You shouldn't be parked here."

"Oh? Why not?"

"This is a recent trail. You need to stay on the established roads, or in one of the established camp sites."

"OK. I saw the fire ring here and figured this was established." I didn't want to be confrontational since this guy was wearing a tactical belt with pepper spray and a handgun. Alright, I wouldn't provoke him even without that stuff: he was a big guy. But come on, people had been driving in here and camping - what was I to think when I saw it? *Oh, there's a nice shady campsite, I think I'll avoid it.*

"Well, this is *newly* established," he explained.

I was OK with them trying to keep the area as pristine as possible, but I was slightly annoyed that this guy was busting *my* chops. It's not like I was the person who blazed the new trail and built the fire ring. Plus, the ranger himself just now drove *his* truck down the trail. So I asked him to explain to me which areas were established and which areas were *newly* established, under the guise of not wanting to make the same mistake again. He launched into a lengthy explanation, punctuated by points of reference and areas of particular interest. I interrupted him a few times for clarification, although I am quite familiar with the area. "So, it's OK to drive down the road to the left of the big rock, but not make a new trail to the right?" I would ask.

Finally the guy got flustered and left. I am sure that the next time I am in that area the *newly* established campsite will be much more established because the ranger didn't bother to block the trail with rocks or tree branches, let alone put up a sign to indicate the area was closed.

Can't You Hear Me Knocking?

We returned to the mountain cabin on the first Saturday of August. I geared up as quickly as possible and was on the river by 12:45. While climbing down the precipitous river bank I slipped on the loose dirt and rocks and slid a good 25 feet on my backside, bouncing over large rocks and banging into logs before finally coming to rest. I laid there for several minutes looking at the sky through the trees, waiting for something to start hurting or bleeding, and was amazed when it didn't. *Well, that's one way to get down to the river quickly.* Except I had to climb back up the acclivity to retrieve my rod from where I had dropped it at the start of my fall.

I began with a rubber-legged attractor followed by a Yellow Sally. My very first cast into a shallow riffle just off shore enticed a small nine-inch brown to hit the Yellow Sally, which I hooked, landed and released successfully. Yellow-colored dry flies seemed to be the ticket today, and I also had luck with Pale Morning Duns. I caught five fish in all, one a decent-sized 12-inch brown, but most were little nine-inchers, including one that was determined to be a pain in my ass. Before I could remove the hook from its mouth it squirted out of my hand and jumped back in the river, but it didn't go far because in the process it managed to wrap the leader around my rod. "Come back here, you little prick," I said as I re-netted him, miffed that I would have a tangle to deal with. I removed the hook and released him, then reattached the net to the magnetic catch on my chest-pack shoulder strap.

I went to work untangling my line, but before too long I felt a short series of tugs that seemed to come from my net. It is not unusual for my ridiculously massive net to come detached from the magnetic hook, either because it gets snagged on vegetation or the current pulls at it when I'm in the river, which I assumed was the case this time. I glanced over my shoulder to see that the net was still attached, and that it was hanging above the surface of the water. *Hmm, weird.* I went back to the tangle, only to feel the net tug again. *OK, what the heck is going on?* I reached back and unlatched my net and took a look inside. There in the bottom of the stupidly deep net was the fish I thought I had released! It must have swam right back into my net without my realizing it. After some revival I released the fish, this time well away from Giganto-net.

No Deposit, No Return

Kathy and I decided to hike Sunday morning, hopeful to find somewhere we hadn't been before. Looking at the national forest map, and then at the more precise topo map, we decided to try a trail which I am not going to name for fear of being sued. You'll understand shortly. This hike didn't appear in any of the local guide books, but it looked like it followed a creek, gently gaining elevation from the valley floor and up into the mountains. Once we found the trailhead and parked the truck, we walked uphill for a quarter mile before coming to a gate across the trail and a homemade sign demanding money for crossing a half mile of private property. Maybe this was why the hike wasn't listed in any guide book. The fee was $1 per human, and $2 for each four-legged creature such as dogs and horses. I'm not sure what you would do if you had a three-legged dog - pay $1.50 I guess.

Despite the cheesy sign, this guy had official-looking pre-printed envelopes and a secure drop box to deposit the extortion money, I mean land-use fee. But who hikes with their wallet? And I sure as hell wasn't going to make the half mile round-trip trek back to the truck to walk through a half mile of supposed private property that looks from more than one map like public land. "We'll pay on the way back," I lied.

Kathy said, "I have two dollars in my pocket." Somehow Kathy always has a few dollars on her. Just in case we stumble upon happy hour out on one of these trails I guess. So I dutifully, but very reluctantly put the two dollars into the envelope and dropped it into the box. Just so I felt like we were getting our money worth I stepped behind a tree and took a whiz on this guy's property, wishing all along I could leave a bigger "deposit."

Before very long the trail looked down on a ranch house and a few out-buildings that I assumed belonged to the people whose land we were supposedly crossing. We actually saw a guy far below, walking away from one of several ponds on the property with a fishing rod in his hand, but he paid no attention to us whatsoever. It looked like a beautiful piece of land that bordered a tumbling creek, facing up the valley toward the high mountain peaks. With a place like that I'm not sure why he needed to squeeze out a dollar here and there from hikers. Of course it is entirely possible that this land is not owned by the people who own this ranch, but someone else. (I put that part in at the last minute to decrease my chance of being sued by the fishing-rod ranch guy. I hope it works!)

We hiked in and out of the trees for a couple of hours, the trail generally following the creek, but never really running alongside of it like we hoped. Finally the trail did veer *close* to the creek, so we stepped off and found a log to sit on and ate our lunch while overlooking the rushing water. After lunch the sky began to look threatening, and with no clear destination in mind we decided to hike out. But we had only taken a few steps back when we came upon a guy hiking in. It turns out he had hiked this trail before and said there were some pretty cool places up ahead. So we turned around and continued our trek and were glad we did. We came to a narrow rock passageway that overlooked the creek as it flowed through a deep gorge, and beyond that some picturesque beaver ponds fed by tumbling cascades in an unusually verdant spot. Eventually we turned around and hiked back out the way we came, estimating we had gotten about six miles of scenic exercise for the day and had made some nice memories.

Eighteen and I Like It

The following weekend we drove up to the mountain place again on Saturday morning, but this time daughter Megan, her husband Bronson and our grandkids were there to greet us, having driven up Friday evening. Fortunately there were no mice waiting for them when they arrived, or any sign of mice all weekend.

Kathy and Megan took the kids to the annual Gold Rush Days celebration at the Buena Vista town park for the afternoon. I was finally able to get Bronson out on the river after giving him a fly rod for Christmas. This would also be the first time he would wear his brand new, much-nicer-than-mine wading boots that he bought at the Sportsman's Expo in January.

Todd, Laurie and their son Trevor were also in Chaffee County for the weekend, so Bronson and I drove the eight miles upstream to meet Todd. He had arranged for us to fish his cross-stream neighbor's property - the same pristine land Todd and I fished back in early May. The three of us drove upstream a couple more miles to the bridge across the river, and then back downstream a few miles to our host's vast river frontage. Once we parked the truck we walked another 15 minutes to the river where Todd rigged Bronson's brand-new fly rod with a double-nymph set-up. This would be Bronson's first time doing some serious fly fishing other than when he was a kid generally foiling his Dad's attempts to catch trout. Todd gave Bronson some instruction and within 30 minutes of his first cast he caught a fish, whereby Todd declared that Bronson needed no further guidance and bolted upriver. We only saw Todd one other time the rest of the day, and only then because he lost his dry-fly floatant. He walked several hundred yards downstream to reclaim the "Jet-Fuel" floatant he had presented to me as a gift earlier in the day. I didn't much care for the stuff anyway.

An hour or so later Bronson yelled upstream to me that he had caught another fish, holding up his sagging net as proof. I reeled in my line, set my rod down and hustled downstream to help him release it. When I looked into the net I was stunned at what I saw. Brand-new fly fisherman Bronson, with his brand-new rod and brand-new boots had hooked and landed a fat 18-inch rainbow trout! It took me four years of fly fishing before I caught anything this big, and that was earlier this year when I caught Bowzilla on this same property. Todd says it took him two years to catch any fish at all. And here Bronson caught a monster within two hours of stepping into the river. I grabbed the fish and removed the fly, but the instant the fly was out of its mouth the damn fish leapt from the net and swam away, thwarting our attempt at the photo op. I felt terrible that I let the fish get away, but Bronson, being the true sportsman, said he was just glad that I was there to witness his trophy.

We worked our way upstream, and Bronson caught another fish, giving him a total of three for the day. I'm not sure how long it took me to catch three fish in a day, perhaps a few years. It certainly wasn't on my first time out. Eventually Bronson tired though, as I saw him just sitting on the bank a few times. When I had the chance to ask if he was alright he said he was enjoying the serenity of the river - peace and quiet being a rare commodity to the father of four-year-old and seven-month-old kids.

I wound up having a banner day on the river, catching almost twice as many fish as my previous best of six, achieved several weeks earlier. In five hours of fishing this day I caught 11 fish, mostly browns of about 9-11 inches, but a couple measured 12-13 inches, along with an occasional rainbow. Three or four times during the course of the day, after fishing a run that had been unproductive, I decided to cast one last time before moving on, only to catch a fish on that final cast. In one instance I hooked a nice 13-inch brown on a large, yellow-bodied, Elk Hair Caddis dry fly, and as I was trying to land him I saw two other smaller fish swarming around. Before I knew what was happening one of them struck the second fly, a Copper John nymph, and I had two fish on my line at once. *Well this is a new one.* I concentrated on landing the first, bigger fish, but the smaller fish, perhaps 10 inches, insisted on coming along for the ride. After I netted the first one I also managed to scoop the second one into my giganto-net, where the two fish behaved well together until I removed their flies and sent them on their way.

If I caught 11 fish, I knew Todd would have caught a lot more. Once he showed up back at the truck, a good 15 minutes beyond our agreed-upon time, I asked him how many he had caught. I was not surprised when his response was, "Twenty."

We all met at Laurie and Todd's place for dinner that night, a chance to bid farewell to nephew Trevor, who would be leaving for his freshman year at an out-of-state college in a few days. Laurie provided appetizers out on the riverside deck, but in a moment of inattention an opportunistic chipmunk helped himself to the snacks, leaving a "calling card" behind and soiling the rest of the goodies. Fortunately Kathy had brought enough of her signature lasagna to more than fill us up.

After dinner we sat around a rivers-edge campfire and roasted marshmallows and made s'mores while laughing about good times past, present and yet to come. A few kayakers silently paddled by, guided by the light of the full moon. I quietly commented about how that was the local kayak club on their monthly full-moon, naked paddle. Todd shattered the hushed reverie by shouting after the kayakers, "HEY! ARE YOU NAKED?"

Hang 'em High

The traffic to and from the mountain place, particularly driving back to metro Denver on Sundays, has been so bad that we have been altering our schedule so that we can drive back on Monday mornings. There has been no official word on why the two-hour drive is now a stop-and-go three hours, but personally I think it is because traffic along I-70 to the north is so horrendous that more people are recreating further south just to avoid I-70. To compensate for coming home a half-day later, we have been leaving Denver for the mountains a half-day later. And surprisingly traffic seems no worse heading up to the mountains on Saturday morning than on Friday afternoon.

On this Saturday, the final one of August, I donned an old pair of jeans, a long-sleeve t-shirt, gloves, safety glasses, a dust mask and a hard hat for a fun-filled adventure in the crawl space beneath the cabin. My mission, which I accepted very reluctantly, was to crawl around on my knees, trying not to hit my head on the low-hanging beams, get bit by black-widow spiders or attacked by rabid badgers, and spray nasty poison in the enclosed space in an attempt to slow the carpet beetle invasion in the bug room. After what seemed like at least two hours of coughing, hacking and expletive-laced head-bonking I had enough and crawled out for some fresh air. I asked Kathy how long I had been down there and she thoughtfully responded, "I don't know, maybe 20 minutes."

After blowing enough nasty bug-spray crap out of my nose to fill an oil tanker, I headed for the river, where I fished for three hours without landing a fish. The water level was less than half of what it had been two weeks ago, as the water managers enacted the annual mid-August flow reduction from upstream reservoirs. I did hook a large fish early that hit a hopper imitation, but after ten or fifteen seconds he broke free. In trying to analyze what I did wrong, all I could think was that perhaps I didn't keep my rod tip up high enough. I hate when that happens. I had another fish jump out of the water when my lower fly inadvertently got stuck behind a rock that I had casted over, leaving my upper fly suspended about 18 inches above the surface of the water. Unfortunately the fish didn't jump high enough to reach it, and it didn't try again, even though I gave it plenty of opportunity by letting it hang there for 30 seconds or so.

Hairy Legs and Bloody Stumps

After a little more carpet-beetle-mitigation work Sunday morning, this time above ground, I headed out to fish the river further upstream than yesterday, hoping the earlier hour and cooler water would change my luck. I found a new-to-me road pull-out near the water I wanted to fish, but still walked 15 minutes at a healthy pace before reaching the river. Once there I had to untangle a freaking mess before I could make my first cast. Am I the only angler that dutifully secures his fly to the hook-keeper on his rod, only to find a Titanic-sized glob of tangled line after walking to the river?

When I finally made a cast a fish came up to check out my hopper, but refused it. This was very good-looking water so I was surprised when I went an hour without any more activity. Finally I had a strong hit and a hearty fight, but the fish got off. I couldn't figure out what I did wrong this time. Perhaps a poor hook-set? Eventually I did catch a couple of fish on droppers, the first taking a Flashback Pheasant Tail and the second a Prince Nymph.

At one point during the day I got my foot wedged between a couple of under-water rocks while wading. It was stuck enough that I started to think I was going to have to cut it off with my keychain-pocket knife. But Kathy always has a good idea where I'm fishing, so once I missed dinner she probably would have suspected something was wrong and sent someone after me. At least I'd like to think so. It hadn't occurred to me to simply untie my boot and pull my foot out. What did occur to me was to kneel down and move the offending rocks away from my foot, which was a little more difficult than it sounds since they were pretty big rocks under a few feet of water, but probably a lot easier than hacking through my ankle with a dull pocket-knife.

As I was changing out flies on the bank a little later I heard a crashing noise just downstream, and looked up in time to see a rather large tree branch smash to the ground where I had been standing just moments before. It wasn't big enough to kill me, I don't think, but it sure would have ruined my day. Particularly if I was down to just one foot and a bloody stump.

I switched out the upper hopper for something that would support more weight below. I chose a huge, orange, foam, hairy-legged thing and attached a double-bead head golden stone fly below that. Still nothing. So I switched out the dry for an indicator, left the Golden Stone, and tied a Copper John on the bottom. And in quick succession I caught two fish, one on each of these flies. I had a hell of a time getting the second fish in the net. I brought him in as far as I could, but when the line-to-leader perfection loop got hung-up on my tip-top guide, I still had 12 feet of leader and tippet extending from my rod tip. And no matter how far I stretched my rod-arm upstream I couldn't reach the fish with my net-arm extended downstream. After several minutes the fish finally figured *Ah, to hell with it* and swam into the net just to get it over with.

I had more work to do back at the house and couldn't fish all day, so when I snagged a tree on my back cast and lost my whole rig I decided that was my sign to head home. Even though the day had its frustrations, such as only catching four fish when I knew there were a ton of them swimming all around me, I still caught four fish. Plus I didn't see another soul for the entire three hours, until a couple of kayakers came paddling downstream just as I was climbing up the bank for the walk back to the truck.

Semi-Gross

On our last trip to the mountain house I had taken a water sample from an indoor faucet, which originates from a well on the property. We have not been drinking the water for a couple of years because it plays havoc on the digestive tract of some of us (mainly me). But recently myself and the occasional guest have had some unpleasant symptoms simply from brushing teeth and eating fruit washed in the household water. When showering, the water has always smelled a little gnarly, which I attributed to the fact that it is natural well-water with dirt and sand and whatever else comes up from the ground with the water. Anyway, I went to the county environmental health office to pick-up a water-test kit, which consisted simply of a small plastic cup and instructions saying to send the sample and $20 to *another* Colorado county for testing. And by the way, it has to arrive there within 30 hours of taking the sample, which means another $20 or so to overnight it.

We got the test results back within a few days and learned that while the water has no ecoli bacteria, there is a high level of coliform bacteria. The recommended solution is to sanitize the well and the household pipes with chlorine bleach, and to possibly replace the well cap with a sanitary-seal cap. When we got to the mountain place the first Saturday in September I climbed down to the well head, which is located in the spidery basement of a small shed on the property, to inspect the well cap and to take photos for anyone who may be able to help us with replacing it. I did learn that the well is 44 feet deep and ground water is just 26 feet down, according to notes I found scribbled on the pressure tank. While I was down there I also removed a dead chipmunk, whose guts had apparently dried up because when I went to chuck it across the road his otherwise-intact body hardly had enough weight to fly four feet. Rather than plopping down with a thud on the other side of the road, it just barely cleared the short property fence I was standing next to, where it slowly drifted to earth and landed with an inaudible puff.

I guess this was my day for dead-rodent chucking, because there were also three mice caught in traps in the house. This was certainly a disappointment to Kathy and me because we thought we had the mouse situation under control. I am always amazed at how dead mice can emit such a powerful, nasty smell. You would think that the disgusting odor would be enough to warn their buddies away, but obviously not.

By the time I made it to the river it was about 3 p.m. I fished for a few hours, catching just two fish, both within moments of each other, on nymphs. I unfortunately had to leave the fly, about a number 16 Golden Stone, in the second fish's mouth. I had no luck at all on dry flies, unless you consider success to be one looky-loo and one tepid but missed strike. I headed for the truck when I finally decided it just wasn't my day, but as soon as I reached the flat ground above the river channel, I looked down at my feet to see a big, steaming pile of bear crap, loaded with plenty of undigested-looking berries. At first I wasn't sure what it was, but after tasting it I realized, *yep, bear crap*. Not really of course. But after looking at it for a few moments I decided I probably shouldn't hang around too long. The walk back to the truck through the piñons in the twilight was quiet, lonely and a little eerie. Later research confirmed my suspicion that what I had seen, actually almost stepped in, was indeed bear crap.

Flaky

After looking at a local zoning map, I went upstream the following day to fish an area marked as BLM land – Bureau of Land Management - that I had not previously explored. After parking at a campground I walked upstream a quarter mile or so to get beyond water that probably saw a lot of fishing pressure from campers. I fished for several hours and did not catch a single fish. Oh sure, I got the usual rise to my very first cast, but did not hook the fish. If they kept statistics for everything in fly fishing like they do baseball, I would probably see that I'm 2-24 on days that I miss the first strike. I'm not sure why I get shutout so often after missing that first strike. Either the fish have one hell of a grapevine, or I have some awfully bad mojo. It probably didn't help that shortly after that first miss I lost my rig in a tree, and after spending some time tying on new tippet and two flies, I got the whole thing hopelessly tangled on my very next cast.

After a couple of hours of frustration I came upon a grizzled old guy with a long, white beard and a big, floppy, felt hat who looked like he should be panning for gold in 1872. When he got closer we exchanged pleasantries, and I noticed he was indeed carrying a gold pan. He said the river was loaded with gold, but small flakes. He also said he had been catching his limit of fish in this water for the last several days. I should have asked if his fish were as small as his gold flakes.

Old Man, Look at my Life

Mid-to-late September is our favorite time of the year in Chaffee County, so we try to spend as much time at the mountain place as we can. The weather is generally outstanding, with crisp, calm days and clear, cool nights. And of course the aspen trees put on a stunning multi-colored display. But I awoke on the second Saturday of the month with a bad cold that had given me no warning it was coming. Twelve hours later it hit Kathy, and a prime weekend was spent mostly sick in bed. So we set an ambitious schedule for September's third weekend, planning to disinfect the well, go on a four-wheel drive autumn-color photography trip and of course get some fishing in. We pulled in Friday evening to get an early Saturday start on sanitizing the well, and were finished with that responsibility by noon. Since we couldn't use the water until we drained the disinfecting bleach from the system after 24 hours, we arranged to spend the night with Laurie and Todd at their place.

Todd and I walked out his back door early Saturday afternoon to fish the river. For some reason I was feeling confident in my fishing abilities and so decided for the first time ever to fish three flies at once. I regretted it almost immediately. I had only cast the dry fly and two-dropper rig a couple of times before it became massively tangled, and I had to retreat to the river's edge to try and save my leader and re-rig with something more manageable. We worked our way upstream for about four hours, until about 5 p.m., in which time I managed to catch just three fish.

Kathy and I planned to drive up and over Weston Pass to photograph the fall scenery on Sunday. But we woke up to heavy overcast skies and light rain, and the forecast called for more of the same the entire day. So even though this initially looked to be the prime weekend for autumn landscape photography, we decided the conditions were less than ideal and opted to wait for better weather the next weekend - when hopefully the trees wouldn't be too far beyond their colorful peak. I felt bad for Kathy because she really looks forward to getting out on sunny fall days and discovering different places to take photos of the changing leaves, and her enthusiasm shows in her stunning photographs.

The weather was not so bad, however, that we couldn't fish. Todd and I walked upriver along the dirt road to begin fishing where we had stopped yesterday. But before we could we needed to wade across to the other side where we had permission to fish. The river at this point is not as easy to cross as it is behind Todd's place, but it's not terribly difficult this time of year either. Unfortunately I did have some trouble wading to the opposite bank thanks to the lingering effects of my cold and the influence it had on my energy level. When I was halfway across I stopped to rest and Todd was either worried for my safety or impatient for me to get out of the water he wanted to fish, because he waded out to help me to the other side. I appreciated his help, but it made me feel like an old man - a designation I am not yet willing to accept.

We fished for three or four hours in which time I caught seven fish on blue-colored nymphs. As we worked our way upstream I came across a promising run along the shore, but the only way I saw to fish it was by climbing on top of a big boulder. From my vantage point eight feet above the water I saw a good-sized fish move out into the flow to inspect my nymph as it drifted by. The fish refused it so I tried a second time, and again it took a look but didn't strike. I decided to try a third and final time and this time the fish hit it. Somehow I was able to land this fat, 17-inch brown trout with relative ease - for some reason it just wasn't as difficult to net as some smaller fish I have caught. This was a rare occasion when I was upstream of Todd, having passed him while he was eating a sandwich. He walked upstream to take my photo with this prize, but when I held it up it slipped out of my hands and splashed into the river, where it lodged under some rocks with the hook still in its mouth - and refused to budge.

We teamed up to coax it from its safe haven and with some difficulty re-netted it. I was smart enough this time to remove the fly before holding it up for the hero photo, and sure enough as soon as I held it up it squirmed free once again, falling in what seemed to be slow motion as I clumsily made a futile attempt to catch it, before it splashed down and swam away vigorously.

At this point Todd began fishing upstream from me, probably so he would have first crack at some of these productive runs. But before long he was well above me, working his way quickly upriver. Before we had left the house, he agreed with Laurie that he would return by 2:15 p.m. for their drive home to metro-Denver. I kept an eye on my watch, and as zero-hour approached I purposely began moving faster in an attempt to catch up with Todd, because for some reason he relies on me to tell him the time. I have no idea why he doesn't wear a watch, or why he doesn't check his phone for the time every once in a while. And what does he do when he's fishing alone? Go all mountain-man and tell time by the position of the sun? In any event, I was pretty worn down from my cold by this time, and I didn't have the energy to race upstream over rocks, around boulders and through the brush just to tell Todd the time. Eventually he came walking downstream to where I was and asked me the time. "2:45," I answered.

"2:45!? Crap, why didn't you tell me?"

"Because I couldn't catch up to you."

"Damn it, I was supposed to be back 30 minutes ago!" he yelled over his shoulder as he bolted downstream.

"Don't blame me Todd," I shouted after him. "It's not my fault you don't wear a watch."

As houseguests of Todd and Laurie, Kathy and I had an obligation to be out of their house by the time they were, so I also hustled down the shore toward the house, which was about a mile away. But before long Todd was around the bend and out of site. I moved as quickly as I could, but was tiring easily thanks to my persistent cold. By the time I got to the place where we had waded across the river that morning I was exhausted. I sat on a rock and caught my breath, thinking that I would gladly accept some help now, even if it meant admitting to being an old man. The only other choice was to continue downstream and make the easier crossing right at Todd and Laurie's place, but the thought of walking another half mile down the rocky river bank was less appealing than taking my chances here and then walking down the dirt road. Besides, it wasn't like I was trying to cross Victoria Falls. The worst that could happen was that I would take a spill into the chilly water before regaining my footing. But I chose my path carefully and actually had an easier time crossing than I did in the morning. Once up on the dirt road I hustled back to the house, walking up to see Todd and Laurie hurriedly packing their car for departure and Kathy loading our overnight gear into our truck. I said goodbye to Laurie and thanked her for her hospitality, but Todd and I did not speak before I drove off with Kathy.

Once back at the house we opened all the faucets and drained the bleachy water from the pipes. The following morning we dutifully collected another sample and sent it off for testing. We received the disappointing results a couple of days later: the coliform levels were still very high.

Sore-Ass Pass

We drove up to the mountains again the following weekend, hopeful that the fall colors would still be abundant. Saturday was a gorgeous day with blue skies, sunshine and white, puffy clouds, so we drove toward Leadville and then pulled off the highway and headed up Weston Pass. The road turned from pavement to well-maintained, graded-dirt that became rougher and rockier as it progressed toward the 11,921 foot summit. It was still an easy drive, but I did notice one or two places that could damage some vehicles.

The aspen leaves were bright gold at the lower elevations, but as we climbed higher the trees had already begun to lose their leaves, and those that remained were less vibrant. Even though we were about one week late for the prime colors, we did get some decent photos at the lower elevations. Still, we continued toward the summit since we had never been here before, just to see what we would see.

Near the summit on both the west and east sides were some old, dilapidated log cabins. But because a lot of people were out on this beautiful day, photographing them in a more or less natural state was a challenge. The road on the east side of the pass was quite wide and smooth, obviously better maintained by Park County than the west side was by Lake County. But there were very few aspen trees on the east side, and without stopping for photography we made it down in short order.

Eager to continue the outing, I talked Kathy into proceeding to Breakneck and Brown's Passes, hopeful to find more aspen gold. Unfortunately both of these roads - that went basically nowhere - were mostly in the thick forest, not allowing for much of a view beyond the trees that surrounded us. And the ride was bone-jarring. I guess the name Breakneck should have been a clue, although a better name may be Sore-Ass Pass, or perhaps Ache-Back Road to Freaking Nowhere. At one point we did come across an old mine ruin, but it was less than photogenic and certainly wasn't worth the trouble getting there.

Wile E. Coyote

Like last week, this Sunday morning was very threatening with a thick layer of dark-gray clouds covering the sky. Kathy and I took a walk, covered the swamp cooler for the season and generally took it easy. After lunch, I went to buy some flies based on a conversation with Todd when he said he caught 25 fish Friday on blue and purple prince nymphs and just about anything with a lot of flash. But being the cheapskate I am, I didn't go to the fly shop, but rather an outdoor-oriented merchandise store where the flies are half the cost of fly-shop flies. But unfortunately they didn't have anything blue or purple, so I stocked up on a few other patterns. When I walked out of the store the weather was clearing, making me anxious to get on the river, so I stupidly did not go to the fly shop to look for blue and purple patterns.

After a 10 minute drive and walking briskly for another 10 minutes to get to the river, I did find one purple nymph left in my box from last weekend. I tied that on below a larger, flashy prince nymph, but realized I was in trouble after fishing this for an hour without a single strike. I thought about calling it a day, because it felt like one of those days when the fish were just not interested. But by now the sun was breaking through the clouds on occasion, and the golden leaves falling from the trees and floating lazily onto the water made for a compelling setting and provided me with some motivation to stick around a little longer. I switched flies, still without any interest from the fish. I changed the depth I was fishing, I changed flies again, I even changed to a different color indicator.

At one point I was half-sitting on and half-leaning against a boulder along the bank while changing flies. When I finished and got up from my rock perch the whole boulder shifted with an enormous, echoing rumble and thundered down the bank toward me. Once again, in my moment of need, my mouth involuntarily spit out a string of expletives that would make a construction-working, hip-hop musician envious. Like Wile E. Coyote, I idiotically tried to outrun it instead of simply dodging to one side. It only took a second for the giant rock to catch up to me, where it came to rest against the back of my leg, pinning my right heel beneath it. *Great. There is no way I'm getting out of this mess with anything less than a broken heel.* But when I took stock of the situation I realized that only the heel of my boot was stuck. After a few minutes of struggling I was able to pull my foot free. This time I quickly jumped to one side in case the big-ass rock decided to continue its downward trek to the river, but thankfully its travels were over.

Finally after three hours of not even seeing a fish, I changed to a big terrestrial dry fly and a Flashback Pheasant Tail nymph, and then watched as a fish swam over to take a look. *Well, that's more action than I've seen all day.* Unless you count getting chased by an enormous, evil rock. I was encouraged that a fish showed some interest, and at the same time discouraged that it wasn't interested enough to eat the fly. But by now the sun was finally out and I hoped that this somehow meant the fish would become more active. Ten minutes later I thought I detected a strike so I set the hook. But when I felt no resistance I let the fly continue to drift downstream. When I picked it up to cast again there was a fish on the line - just a small fingerling, about four or five inches long. I tried to shake it off the hook but it didn't come free, leaving me with the trouble of unhooking and releasing it. Once again I was encouraged and discouraged at the same time. I fished for another 20 minutes or so without even a hint of fishly interest before finally climbing out of the river and walking back to the truck. To add insult to injury, when I took my waders off I found that my right leg and foot were soaking wet, indicating a hole somewhere in the waders.

Stinky Town

I would like to preface this story by saying that I have greatly enjoyed the time I have spent in Wyoming throughout my life. There are plenty of wide-open spaces, traffic jams are pretty much unheard of - unless you happen to get stuck behind a bison wandering down the middle of the road - and the few people who live there are generally incredibly friendly.

Case in point: I had business in a mid-sized Wyoming town (pop. 10,000) several years ago and immediately after it was concluded my wife and I drove toward Yellowstone National Park for a vacation. After only driving about 15 miles we stopped in a tiny town (population 350) for dinner at a highly recommended restaurant. Unfortunately I didn't notice the NO CREDIT CARDS sign prominently displayed at the entrance. We greatly enjoyed a fabulous dinner and of course when it came time to pay for our meal I whipped out the plastic. When our server saw the credit card she politely informed us of the restaurant's policy. "Well, that's a bit of a problem," I responded. For reasons that escape me now, we didn't have enough cash to pay for the meal and didn't have a checkbook with us.

The waitress turned instantly sullen and said, "I'll ask the owner to come have a chat with you," in such an ominous tone that I expected to be escorted out to the alley and have my legs broken before being tossed into the dumpster.

The owner appeared at our table presently, making us wait just long enough for me to break into a sweat. "How was your meal?" he asked congenially. *Maybe this won't be so bad after all.*

"Delicious," I said, while my wife simultaneously responded, "Wonderful."

"Then why are you refusing to pay?"

Gulp. "We aren't refusing sir, it's just that all we have is a credit card."

"I see. So you didn't see the giant NO CREDIT CARDS sign at the door?"

"Well, umm...we heard so many great things about your restaurant, and were so excited to come in that we must have missed it."

"Well you have three options. One: we can call the cops. Two: you can both wash dishes for four hours tonight, or three: you can send me a check when you get home," he said, breaking into a big smile.

"We'll take option three," my wife and I said together.

"Ha ha. That seems like the best choice," he laughed while slapping me on the back. "Glad you enjoyed your meal. Here's my card. Thank you for coming!"

Of course the first thing we did when we got home was send the restaurant a check, and I have had fond feelings for Wyoming ever since. Unfortunately what follows would put those feelings to the test.

Todd called me on the first Thursday of October to see if I wanted to join him, a buddy and the buddy's stepson this weekend to fish a central-Wyoming river. It seems that a fourth guy had to cancel late, so Todd invited me to go the day before the departure date. Apparently the buddy fished here regularly and would show us the ropes. I accepted the invitation, not so much because I was looking forward to two days in a small car with Todd and his pals, or sharing a hotel room with Todd for three nights, or even the two days fishing a new place. I agreed to go because I thought it might be enjoyable to write about the experience. Before I begin writing about it in earnest let me just say that this better be as much fun as a bachelor party on steroids - because the trip was brutal.

After I agreed to go, Todd asked if I would mind calling the fly shop nearest our destination and ask them a series of very specific questions so that he could make sure we had with us the correct flies, leader and tippet without actually having to buy them from the store that was offering the advice. Among the questions I agreed to ask:

- Required fishing license(s) & cost?
- How is the river fishing?
- Clarity/CFS?
- Recommended dry flies/nymphs/streamers?
- Recommended leader & tippet size?
- Monofilament vs. fluorocarbon tippet?

I called the fly shop on their toll-free number and the woman who answered said she couldn't hear me, so I told her I would call back. In the meantime I got busy, so after a while I typed an email with Todd's questions and sent it off to the address listed on the fly shop's web site. Several hours later I hadn't heard back, so when I had a few minutes I called the fly shop back - this time on my dime ($1.29 actually) - and reached the same woman as before, who said she could hear me fine this time. I was tempted to suggest she get her toll-free line fixed, but thought better of it. I proceeded to ask all of Todd's questions, which the woman graciously answered, although she seemed a little baffled about why I would be calling instead of simply stopping in when we got there. After our conversation concluded, I emailed her responses to Todd, who in turn replied, "I would suggest we buy local flies. Patterns can differ from one area to the next. Buy their tippet and leader as well." *If we were going to just stop in*

and buy their stuff, like any sane person would do, why did I
spend half a day trying to get a hold of these people?

Since my waders had developed a leak that I wanted to repair prior to the trip, I then drove to the local fly shop for a tube of Aqua Seal. Upon returning home I found a single hole, although it looked a little small to allow so much water into my waders. I repaired the hole, just barely leaving the recommended 24 hours for it to cure before our anticipated 5 p.m. Friday departure time.

Not wanting to be the guy who brought along two tons of crap, I spent a fair amount of time Friday pairing down my gear and clothes so it would all fit into a small gear bag and a smaller duffel. When Todd, his buddy Ray and Ray's stepson Lyle pulled up to my place at 5:30 p.m. for the seven-hour drive, a gigantic cooler loaded with beer took up 80 percent of the gear-space in the small SUV. Beer that was not offered to me until Sunday night when it finally became obvious to Ray and Lyle that they could not possibly drink it all by themselves. Luckily Todd had a cargo box mounted on the roof, so my stuff was thrown up there alongside Todd's gigantic gear bag, back-roller pillow, head pillow, body pillow and what I think was a souvenir pillow from the 1904 World's Fair. I guess it's the prerogative of the guy who is driving to bring as much crap as he wants.

Once on the road I learned that Ray and Lyle were spinning fishermen and that Ray was interested to see how a fly fisherman fishes his favorite river. Uh-Oh. First sign of trouble five minutes into the trip. The guy who is supposed to show us the ropes wants to see how we fish this unseen river. 90 minutes down the road it started to get dark, so Todd reached for his glasses and of course couldn't find them. He pulled off the highway and after fifteen minutes of tearing the packed car apart searching for his glasses, he declared victory when he found the glasses case. Unfortunately the case was empty. So I drove for 30 minutes or so to Cheyenne, where we stopped for a bite to eat and another extensive search of the car by Todd for his glasses. This time he found them just where he had put them for quick and easy access: in the driver's-door pocket. Adequately equipped for night driving,

Todd once again took the wheel until we stopped for gas two and a half hours later in Casper.

I offered to drive the next leg, pulling off the interstate onto a lonely two-lane road under a very dark sky. The next one and a half hours were spent nervously scanning the roadside for wildlife. Each time we rounded a curve the headlights would illuminate glowing eyes off in the sagebrush, while antelope and deer lurked along the shoulder of the road. Just as most everyone was dozing off, except me - thankfully, I had to abruptly hit the brakes when something short, light-colored and hairy darted across the road right in front of us. Lyle was the only other person to see it and he said he thought it was a coyote. But he was half-awake in the back seat and didn't get the view I had. I am certain it was my ninth-grade gym teacher Mr. Karsh.

We pulled into a small, dilapidated town at midnight. The roadside sign said it had a population of 600, but glancing around at the abandoned buildings I thought this may have been a bit generous. We were only about 35 miles from our hotel room, but Ray insisted that we stop at the local convenience store for our required Indian reservation fishing license. It turns out Ray has been coming up here at least once a year for 40 years to fish, and had some traditions that he was keen to maintain. The ridiculous ritual of stopping at midnight for a fishing license after driving 6-1/2 hours was another indication that this trip may be a little more than I bargained for.

I was surprised at how busy this convenience store was, considering the late hour and the size of the town. But according to the very talkative clerk Bob, who's sad life story I am now intimately and unfortunately familiar with, this was homecoming night at the local high school. Bob said many of the schools 87 students were stopping in for a can of energy drink, but the customers I saw appeared to be oil-field workers, and their purchases seemed to mainly consist of chewing tobacco. And every single time yet another oil-field worker stepped to the cash register, Bob stopped his story-telling and his filling-out-fishing-license forms by-hand in slow-motion to sell tobacco and start a new monotonous story with his latest customer.

Ray already had his license, having bought an annual one earlier in the year, but Todd, Lyle and I each had to go through the agonizingly slow process. We secretly rolled our eyes at each other every time Bob screwed up the form and had to start again, or told a joke that sucked the first time we heard it 30 years ago, or launched into another sad story about his lonely life. My patience wearing thin, I felt like saying, *Well Bob, if you didn't work the graveyard shift at a convenience store in a town with a population of 600, which you have lived in all your life, maybe you wouldn't be so freaking lonely, and maybe you wouldn't be keeping me from getting to bed right now.* But of course I didn't say that because I'm just too nice of a guy.

Despite the late hour, and driving half the night, and my hurry-the-hell-up grouchiness, I had to laugh when Bob sneezed full-force all over Todd's driver's license just before handing it back to him. This prompted Todd to pull a Kleenex out of his pocket to grab his license with, and then snatch a bottle of hand-wash gel off the store shelf and liberally splurb it all over the license before putting it back in his wallet. A full half-hour after pulling in, we finally left with our two-day Indian reservation fishing licenses in hand and $55 less in our wallets. Except that I used a credit card and when I looked at the receipt after returning home from the trip, I saw that Bob had only charged me 55 cents! Maybe that's the real reason behind Ray's tradition of the midnight, convenience-store, fishing-license moron-a-thon.

After driving alongside a large reservoir and then through the river canyon, we finally got to the hotel at 1 a.m. To check-in we had to endure yet another excruciatingly unhurried process. I am always amazed at how long it takes to check-in to a hotel. What the hell can possibly take so long? I have bought a house in less time than it takes to check-in to a hotel room. The clerks concentrate so hard on their top-secret computer screen, while typing 300 words per minute with such grim demeanor, you would think they are entering a nuclear launch code. I suspect that it takes about 30 seconds to check someone in, and the rest of the time they are shopping for a new cell-phone case on Amazon.com.

While we were waiting and waiting for the desk clerk to complete our transaction, we had plenty of time to look around the lobby, which at one time looked like it may have been more than just the wide spot in the hallway that it is now. But now every available nook was filled with mounted hunting trophies – scores of them - including very large animals like grizzly and polar bears. Every cranny had several bloody photos of someone killing a grizzly or polar bear, caribou, crocodile, yak, you name it. From where we teetered half-awake in the narrow lobby, we could see hundreds of these photos lining the walls. And we had time to examine almost all of them in detail while the clerk continued madly typing away.

Just when we thought she was almost done, she produced several drink coupons for the bar, and encouraged us to use them right that instant. When we explained how tired we were and just wanted to get to bed, she told us how their hot tub could soothe our aching muscles, and that we could use our drink coupons to take drinks out to the hot tub. Except, she continued, the hot tub closed at 11. Apparently this rule was not strictly enforced because just as soon as the words were out of her mouth, a young woman wearing a swimming suit and dripping with water came strolling by carrying a tray of cocktails.

In our room at last, Todd and I looked at each other with the same thought. "Not exactly the cleanest place I've seen," he said generously.

"Why is it we're staying here?" I asked.

Todd whispered, "This is where Ray always stays." Ray and Lyle were on the other side of a thin door in the next room.

I was starting to sense that perhaps Ray does things differently than I do. In less than five minutes we were in bed, in less than ten Todd began making the first of his weekend-long groaning sighs, the kind of sound someone would make if a dump truck was parked on their neck.

So despite my exhaustion I did not fall asleep right away. In an effort to drown out moaning Todd with some white noise, and perhaps introduce some fresh air into the moldy-smelling room, I stumbled through the darkness to turn on the window-mounted ventilation unit. But once there I had to retreat back across the sticky carpet to the nightstand for my cell phone so I would have some light to see how to work the thing. Unfortunately it didn't have just a plain fan setting, but rather an air-conditioning setting that should have been labeled "Fairbanks in Winter," and a heat setting that would have been aptly named "Death Valley at 2 p.m. in July." After fiddling with the damn thing for 10 minutes I finally settled on the air-conditioning setting, but with the temperature knob pointing toward the red zone, which either meant "warmer" or "danger." This apparently confused the unit, because it began to emit an odor comparable to a feed-lot where the cows are fed nothing but spoiled mayonnaise. Hopeful that the putrid odor would dissipate within a few minutes, I got back in bed just as Todd awoke from his groaning slumber to ask, "What's that smell?"

"It's the air conditioning," I explained. "It's either going to make it comfortable in here, or burn the whole place down."

Unconcerned, Todd said, "Oh," and rolled over and went back to sleep.

But I still laid there, unable to sleep, thinking about what Kathy had told me. *Don't drink a soda when you stop for dinner. It will keep you awake.* But I didn't heed her advice, thinking that my 7:30 p.m. caffeine would surely be worn off by 1 a.m. And maybe it would have, but I topped off the soda when we left the restaurant and continued to sip it until we made our midnight fishing-license stop. Wide awake and staring at the ceiling, and with the ventilation unit still emitting the pungent stench, I got up once again, this time to shut the damn thing off, suddenly picturing the fungal bacteria that it was undoubtedly harboring and now spewing out all over the room. I later decided the nasty odor is just the normal smell of the whole town, thanks to the nearby hot springs. I later learned the town name is derived from the Greek term for "an odor not dissimilar to that of a big, greasy, steaming pile of crap."

I think I finally dozed off to sleep around 3:30, waking a few minutes before the alarm was set to go off at 7:30. After a sparse continental breakfast at the hotel that was almost suitable for human consumption, and a stop at the nearby grocery store for lunch food, we stopped in at the local fly shop. The small dirt parking lot was crowded with drift boats hooked to vans and a couple dozen middle-aged guys scurrying around in various stages of getting into waders. Unfortunately when we went into the shop we had a difficult time getting any advice regarding flies, leader and tippet as the shop was busy selling stuff to their guide-trip clients. I know these shops make good money from guide-trips, but if they had even *tried* to help us maybe I would be more likely to book a trip with them when I come back. Not that I plan to come back, but more on that later. Finally, based on information gathered by eavesdropping on guide's conversations with their clients, along with the phone conversation of two days earlier, we bought leader and tippet and flies, all of which were much more expensive than any other fly shop I've ever been to.

By 9:30 we had parked the car along the canyon highway, geared up, crossed the road, climbed over the guardrail, half-walked and half-slid down the steep bank and were standing riverside devising a plan. Lyle, who had tossed in a line a few yards away, called, "Check it out!" We looked over in time to see him reel in a 22-inch rainbow trout on his first cast. *Holy Cow! This is going to be a great day.* We all immediately abandoned our plan, hastily spread out a little and casted in. But I was curious how this would play out since as far as I could see the water had none of the features I had been taught to look for as a fly fisherman. It was rather flat water, with no discernable seams, aerated water or fish-hiding rocks. Lyle and Ray continued to catch fish with worms and Rapalas on their spinning reels while Todd and I grew discouraged. At one point one of the drift boats from the fly-shop parking lot came along and fished the opposite bank for about ten minutes, but I didn't see anyone catch anything.

After a while I looked up to see Todd motioning me upstream, where the three of them were crossing over to the other side. This is when I realized that Ray and Lyle were wading across the river in their blue jeans and tennis shoes. This is a wide river through here, maybe 3-4 times as wide as where I'm used to fishing the Arkansas near its headwaters. Luckily they had just reduced the flow at the upstream dam, so with Ray's guidance we were able to cross it without getting in too much above our waist. But I was glad that I was wearing waders and boots and wouldn't be squishing around in wet jeans and tennis shoes the rest of the day like Ray and Lyle.

We walked along the railroad tracks upstream for perhaps a half mile, passing some decent-looking water, before coming to a spot that Ray insisted would produce fish for all of us. Again this water was flat and slow, but there were some large rocks about 20 yards offshore. I could see some big trout swimming around here, and I watched them swim to, but refuse, my flies. Before long I was back to my old tricks of massive tangles, probably from altering my already shaky technique in an attempt to cast further in this wide river than my skill-set allowed.

On the plus side, re-rigging every 10 minutes or so provided an opportunity to try several different flies. Unfortunately these were not the newly-purchased flies of this morning, but rather the Arkansas River flies in my boxes. Todd had taken off with all of our river-specific flies and was moving upriver at warp speed, as is his practice. When Ray recommended we fish our way back downstream, I finally realized that water that is good for spin-fishers to toss night crawlers and lures into is not necessarily good for a fly fisherman to fish tiny flies. I also saw that we were at the mercy of Ray, our self-appointed master-of ceremonies, based on his extensive experience fishing here. I am obviously not a fishing expert, and I appreciated Ray showing us the places where we could wade across this river, but the sudden realization that fishing like a spin-fisher wasn't working for me only added to my frustration. So when I finally caught up to Todd, exhausted from my mostly sleepless night, and hungry from a lack of anything resembling edible, I barked at him in front of Ray and Lyle for taking off with all of our new flies, an outburst which embarrassed everyone, and which I immediately regretted.

And so the day continued, although at one point I did have a nice fish on the line for 10 or 15 seconds before it got off. Ray wound up catching 15 fish for the day with Lyle catching 11. Todd and I were skunked and more than a little miffed that we had come all this way not to catch fish. Heck, I can not catch fish while watching TV in my underwear at home. Once back at the car, Ray informed us that we would have pizza delivered to the hotel room for dinner. Apparently it was a first-night tradition.

"I don't want to mess with your mojo Ray," I started, "but my stomach can't handle the red sauce." And I was starving too. I couldn't eat the fried chicken we bought for lunch because it was too greasy for my stomach. Hell, it was too greasy for the plastic bag it came in, leaching right through it and smearing everything in my waist pack with a slimy coating of oily mucus. I continued, "If no one minds I'll take five minutes on the way back and pick up some tacos or something." No one said anything. It was so quiet that I think I heard some crickets chirping in the car somewhere. I'm still not sure why it was a big deal that I didn't want to eat pizza while sitting on the pubic-hair encrusted hotel-room bedspread stained with dried semen and ass-grease.

Finally Todd said, "Mexican food sounds good, let's stop and get a decent sit-down meal somewhere." More crickets. "I'll buy," Todd added. That seemed to be the key phrase as suddenly everyone was on board.

After a tasty meal and a cold beer we went back to the hotel, where Todd, Ray and Lyle headed for the supposedly natural hot-spring hot tub on the hotel property. Based on the scuziness of the hotel in general, I was fairly concerned about the cleanliness of their hot tub. Alright, I was downright convinced it would be a diseased, pus-filled cesspool. But mainly I was just so tired that I chose instead what I hoped would be a refreshing shower and an early night to bed. But of course the shower was just as grungy as the rest of the place. After unsuccessfully trying to avoid the showers many areas of black, fuzz-covered mildew, I got in bed - after a thorough check of the sheets for anything that crawled - and read for a while before turning the light out.

Having learned my lesson from the vomit-like stench that blasted from the air-conditioning unit, I had the window open this time, despite the sticker on the glass that said in effect: don't open the window because we don't have screens and we don't want bugs in our hotel. Although I'm sure the mice would have appreciated something to eat besides sticky carpet fibers and stale, science-project peanuts that were growing mold under the beds. I drifted quickly to sleep, serenaded by the sounds of Todd moaning and groaning outside in the hot tub. Unfortunately my well-deserved slumber came to a quick and harsh end when Todd opened the door to the room and let out a loud, exaggerated yawn. An overwhelming odor from the hot tub accompanied him, very similar to the aroma of a truckload of spoiled cottage cheese stewing in a giant cauldron of hot asphalt.

Fortunately, Todd showered off the odiferous fetor before hitting the sack, and after several more over-the-top yawns he fell rapidly to sleep. Finally with some quiet and relatively odor-free air, I quickly dozed off as well. But within minutes I awoke to the noise of Todd crying out in pain. "Ahhh...crap! My leg...oh no!" From the sound of it I thought certain he had just been maimed in a rusty-chainsaw accident, so I fumbled for the lamp, turning on the light to see Todd rolled up in a ball, writhing in agony on the bed.

"What's wrong?" I asked, convinced from his gyrations that he was giving birth to a wildebeest.

"Cramp... in...my...groin... ohhhh...crap...ohhhh."

"What can I do?" I asked, horrified that he would ask me to massage it.

Todd suddenly jumped out of bed. "Ohhh...crap," he repeated. He tried to straighten his leg but instead doubled over in pain.

Not having any idea what to do, I said, "Do you want me to take you to the hospital?" I suddenly realized that I had no idea if this town even had a hospital. Surely they had someplace to care for the hundreds of people who were undoubtedly overcome by the town's fumes every year, fumes that at that moment smelled like skunk roadkill being boiled in a mixture of vulture urine and Limburger cheese.

"Ohhh... crap...my groin," came Todd's thoughtful reply as he tried to walk out his cramp.

"Just don't ask me to massage it," I insisted.

"No... my massage therapist says not to massage a cramp," Todd finally said, apparently starting to feel better, but obviously missing the point that I was not about to massage his groin, even if his massage therapist *did* recommend it. After limping and moaning his way around the room for at least half an hour Todd's cramp finally subsided enough for him to get back in bed. I suddenly remembered the earplugs that I had brought along, grabbed them from my bag and jammed them in my ears before turning off the light and sleeping soundly for what remained of the night.

Sunday morning was a carbon copy of Saturday - breakfast, grocery store, fly shop and on the river by 9:30. The only difference is that we were able to coax some advice direct from a fly-shop guide regarding which flies to try. With Lyle and Ray waiting for us in the car, having no need for the fly shop, I discreetly suggested to Todd that perhaps we fly fisherman would have better success if we split up from the spin-fishers and look for more likely fly-fishing water.

Once on the river Todd broke the news to Ray that we were leaving the Ray Show in search of better waters. I tied on a single nymph and did not try to cast further than my skill level and saw immediate results. No, I did not catch a fish - at least not right away - but I didn't have the colossal tangles of yesterday either. That, coupled with the fact that I was fishing the way I knew how - working upstream and in oxygenated water - made me much more comfortable and I was able to relax and enjoy fishing in this very scenic canyon.

In the early afternoon Todd and I came across a wide, relatively shallow stretch of good-looking water peppered with large rocks that showed more potential than anything we had yet fished. Starting along the shore we worked our way out into the river. Suddenly I heard a "whoop" over my shoulder, so I looked across to see Todd fighting what must have been a substantial fish based on the bend of his rod. I immediately reeled in my line and waded over to where Todd was fishing, getting there in time to see him remove the fly from a 20-inch brown trout. I took a quick picture of Todd with the fish before he released it.

"What did it take?" I inquired.

"This psycho nymph. Do you need one?" Todd asked politely.

"No, I have one, thank you." It was quite the courteous exchange after my ill-advised, fly-related conniption of yesterday.

I tied on a psycho nymph as quickly as I could and as I was doing so, Todd caught another big brown. On my second cast with the psycho nymph my indicator took a slight dip so I pulled my rod tip up toward the sky and felt a strong tug. I whistled over to Todd, who yelled, "Keep your rod tip up!" Todd has seen me lose enough fish that he knows my tendencies when I have a fish on the line. But I wasn't about to let this one off. It could be my only fish of the weekend. So I kept the tip up and tension on the line, and I let the fish run a bit here and there before getting its head out of the water. I could see Todd heading toward me out of the corner of my eye, so I decided not to divert my attention from the fish by fumbling with my net. Todd arrived just in time to net the fish for me, a rotund, 19-inch brown trout. After the obligatory photo I released it, anxious to continue fishing this fly in this water. And we fished this water hard, glad to finally find good water and a fly that worked. Todd caught another fish here, a monster 24-incher, but after an hour in this general area without further success we decided it was time to move on.

We did not find such promising water elsewhere, so toward the end of the day, as we were making our way back to the car, we stopped at the productive water once again and fished it for thirty minutes or so without a strike between us. We then walked down the railroad track in the direction of the car and waded back across the river to the highway side. While we were waiting for Ray and Lyle to return from wherever they were, we looked for water nearby that showed any kind of potential. I decided to fish a streamer amongst some rocks along the shore until I grew tired and climbed up the hillside to join Ray and Lyle, who were by now waiting patiently near the car. We sat there for at least 20 minutes watching Todd catch fish in the river below. When he finally stepped out of the water and scrambled up the hill, we learned that he had caught three more fish, one on a streamer and two on dry flies.

Back at the car, Ray announced that the dinner tradition for tonight was to eat at the hotel restaurant. This place could barely put together an edible continental breakfast, but I figured *what the hell, I'll just order a burger. Surely they couldn't mess that up too much.* Once there however, I was almost proved wrong. I ordered a burger cooked medium-well and the waitress said, "I can't guarantee that's how it'll be cooked."

"Excuse me?"

"Well, the cook is a little grouchy tonight," she said, like that somehow made it OK.

"Well, so am I," I responded. "And I can't guarantee that I'll pay for it."

She smiled nervously and finished taking our order. When she finally delivered our meal 40 minutes later - which was puzzling since there were only four other patrons in the entire restaurant - my hamburger was actually pretty tasty. It tasted even better when Ray announced he was buying dinner.

Todd swears that during the course of dinner, although I have no recollection of this and therefore question the validity of his story, I jumped up from the table and began hobbling around the dining room, complaining of a leg cramp. And he brings it up whenever the subject of his massive, middle-of-the-night cramp episode is mentioned. Like somehow my polite, little, standing-up-for two-minutes event, if it even happened, remotely compares to his blood-curdling, hotel-room hysteria.

When it came time to check out Monday morning, Todd left the room charge on the credit card he had used to book the room. And he refused to accept my cash for half of the cost. Todd is either an incredibly nice guy, which come to think of it he mostly is, or he was planning to write off the trip as a business expense since I am a client of his. Or just maybe he wanted to get on my good side so I wouldn't be inclined to hold him responsible in case I contracted some kind of hideous disease from the nasty hotel room.

I enjoy poking fun at Todd because he is a good sport and takes it in good humor. I just hope that he never puts our fishing experiences in writing from *his* viewpoint, because

I'm sure I would be portrayed as a much bigger doofus than I actually am. He would have to work hard at that though, because I'm a pretty big doofus.

As we started our drive back to Denver I requested a quick stop in the river canyon to take a few photos with a camera other than the one on my cell phone. At about 15 miles the canyon is not particularly long, and it is bordered by the highway on one side and active railroad tracks on the other, but it's still photogenic, particularly in the mellow light of morning and late afternoon. Once back on the road, Todd and Ray began making plans for a return trip, mentioning all the different guys who may want to join them. Not once was I mentioned, even though I was sitting right there. Which is OK, I guess, since I have no intention of ever making this trip again. We stopped in Casper for a quick lunch and gas, and being a big spender, I paid for both. The highlight of lunch was when Ray knocked over his 64-ounce drink, effectively making a lake out of the entire, small dining area.

After gassing up, which should have been our last gas stop of the trip, I took a turn behind the wheel. Unfortunately after about 100 miles of driving through a strong crosswind I noticed the automatic transmission was only in fourth gear, one gear below "Drive." My first thought was that Todd, with his long, gangly legs, who was sitting in the front-passenger seat, had somehow bumped the shift lever as he sprawled himself and all his crap out all over the car. But he swears he didn't do it, so of course the suspicion fell on me since I must not know how to drive after 40 years behind the wheel. The bottom line was that we had to stop once again for gas after 200 miles since we had used much more gas than we would have had the car been running at lower rpm. (Full disclosure: a few months afterward I had occasion to drive this car again and paid particular attention to the shift lever. It turns out that in pulling the console-mounted lever straight down from "Park" to the position marked "Drive", it actually lands in 4th gear, which isn't apparent until you look away from the shift lever and up to the dashboard, where the indicator shows '4.' You then have to take the *additional* step of pushing the lever to the right to actually get the transmission into drive. It's a good thing the manufacturer didn't design the brake pedal the same way. *Well yes, it looks like a normal brake pedal, but after you push it once in the center you have to push it again on the right side to actually stop the car.*)

So to summarize: I traveled 850 miles in a small vehicle with long-legged Todd and two guys who never volunteered to drive or pay for gas or share any of their gourmet back-seat munchies such as cashews and smokehouse almonds. Of course I have already groused about their reluctance to share their massive beer supply and all of the space it occupied in the car, despite the fact that I provided all the bottled water for the trip and was more than generous with my beef jerky. (Sounds like a tagline for a porno movie. Cue the cheesy music and the deep-voiced, movie-trailer guy: "He was *more* than generous with his beef jerky.") I spent three nights in a grungy, rancid-smelling hotel room with moaning, groaning, loud-yawning, cramp-prone Todd. What little food I ate tore up my stomach like a garden weasel. I bought a tank of gas that was sucked up twice as fast as it should have been because the car manufacturer is an idiot. And I fished for two days, mostly in water not suitable for fly fishing, all for one freaking fish. Would I do it again? No, not this trip. Was the fun of writing about it worth the experience? Originally the answer was no, but now that a few months have passed I'm beginning to appreciate the absurdity of it all. Did I learn from the experience? Absolutely. I learned never to go fishing - or anywhere really - with Ray, steer clear of Stinkytown Wyoming (not the town's real name of course, but it should be) and avoid sharing a hotel room with Todd, even if he pays. If you are reading this Todd, thanks for inviting me – I had a great time!

Heart of Gold

Friends Clark and Connie accepted our invitation to come up to the mountain house for the final weekend of October. Kathy wanted to get there in plenty of time to clean up any mice messes before they arrived, so we suggested that they come up about noon or so on Saturday. We pulled in by 10:30 Saturday morning but there were no dead mice or mouse crap or odors to deal with. After lunch and hanging around a while I couldn't stand being cooped up any longer on such a beautiful day, so I put on my waders, grabbed my gear and went upstream a mile or so. Kathy said she would text me when Clark and Connie pulled up, so I kept my phone in my chest pocket, protected as always by my fancy waterproof case, more commonly known as a sandwich bag. I checked the phone often in case I didn't hear the texts over the flowing river, but there was no word from Kathy.

Moving up along the bank, I stepped into a little pool that was fed by a small cascade. When I tossed the purple prince nymph into the base of the cascade, my upper dry fly - a ridiculously large and colorful terrestrial thing that was easy to see - was suddenly pulled straight down into the bubbling flow. I set the hook and felt a great deal of resistance. I began to strip line in, but the fish had other ideas. The pull on the other end was strong enough that I realized if I tried to bring the fish in too quick I would lose it, so I let it run. Before I knew what was happening, the fish swam straight for a tiny crevice between two boulders, wedged itself in and refused to budge. It wouldn't move when I tried to strip in line. It wouldn't move when I tried to reel in line. It didn't move when I sat down on a rock and waited for it to get bored and swim out. But after five minutes *I* got bored. I stood up, grabbed a stick, and gently poked it down into the hole, trying to motivate the fish to swim out of its cave. (This sounds horrible, I know. What kind of yahoo jabs at a trapped fish with a stick? But as I saw it my only other option was to cut my line, lose my rig and leave the fly in the fishes lip.) Suffice it to say that standing knee deep in the water, holding my rod high in my right hand, bending down and stabbing a stick into the water with my left hand was not my proudest moment. That's when I heard someone yell.

I turned around to see Kathy at the top of the embankment trying to get my attention. "Clark and Connie are here!" she yelled down to me. A moment later Connie appeared next to Kathy. I felt a little like my sanctuary had been invaded, like when you're a teenager and your Mom unexpectedly barges into your bedroom while you're playing air guitar. "Clark wants to fish at Twin Lakes," Kathy continued. I looked up at Kathy, then into the hole where my fish was still hunkered down. With Kathy and the fish conspiring against me, I admitted defeat. I plunged my arm into the cold water and cut the line as far down as I could reach, and climbed out of the river. In 75 minutes I caught three fish on a purple prince nymph, which Todd had told me had been very successful for him a week earlier. I guess an average of one fish every 25 minutes is OK. Over the course of a typical six-hour fishing outing, that would be 14 fish, which I would certainly be happy with.

Once up at the truck, Clark and I exchanged greetings, and then he transferred his fishing gear from his vehicle to mine. We headed off for Twin Lakes and the women went off somewhere in Clark's car. Clark is one of those big guys with a heart of gold and although we don't have a chance to spend much time together, I always look forward to seeing him. Clark and Connie were friends of Kathy when Kathy and I met, and as a matter of fact Clark sang at our wedding 15 years ago. He has an excellent singing voice that took me by surprise the first time I heard it, which I guess was at our wedding. He just recently retired from his career as a mechanic of very high-end automobiles, and always has great stories about the local Denver-area celebrities - mostly sports stars - whose cars he worked on. Many of these tales revolve around the problems that arise when a $200,000 car is denied routine maintenance, but I could always depend on a few weird anecdotes such as wildly mismatched wheel sizes and odd noises that were simply caused by bizarre stuff bouncing around in the trunk.

As we drove up into Lake County, Clark told me of the fond memories he has of fishing at Twin Lakes with his Dad when he was kid, and admitted he was anxious to recapture some of that childhood nostalgia. He said they mostly puttered around in a small, old boat, trolling for lake trout. We pulled off the highway and headed for the south side of the large lake, for no other reason than it looked more inviting over there near the trees. I was still wearing my waders from fly fishing the river, so what the hell, I waded out into the lake above my knees while Clark quickly rigged up his spinning rod.

We fished quietly for about an hour without any success between the two of us, so we got back in the car and circumnavigated the lake to the far side. We wound up near a huge, humming building that was cordoned off with a barbed-wire topped, chain-link fence. This building obviously had something to do with the lake, so later I did a little research. I found that power is produced here by pumping water out of the lake and uphill to the nearby Forebay Reservoir, then is sucked back down through turbines to generate electricity. I'm sure it's more involved than that, but my mind has a tendency to simplify things for me.

Since we had our back to the big, sucking building, the view in front of us was impressive: the very still lake reflecting the pink sky from the setting sun, framed by the pine-covered mountains. My dry fly/nymph set-up wasn't working at all, so I switched to a streamer, also without success. Once the sun went behind the mountain the fish started to rise, so I switched to a simple Parachute Adams. That didn't work either, and with Clark having the same luck as me, and with the air temperature dropping rapidly, we loaded up the gear and headed out. I told Clark it was too bad we didn't catch any fish and he said that was pretty much how he remembered it as a kid.

Everyone Knows it's Windy

It was rather windy on Sunday morning, but after a delicious, Connie-prepared breakfast we all made a 20-minute drive to Wrights Lake. Clark and I fished of course while the women hiked around and chatted. I caught three rainbows on a rubber-legged terrestrial before losing the fly in the only tree on that side of the lake. As far as I could tell Clark wasn't having much luck on the opposite side of the small lake, so I was glad to see him move over to "my" side. Within short order he caught his first fish of the weekend on the only lure he owns. I switched to a hopper pattern and caught another three rainbows. I was pleasantly surprised that most of the fish were in the 11-inch range, a couple of inches bigger than the little fish I've caught here previously.

The lake is clear enough that you can see the fish swimming over to check out your fly, only to usually swim away, or occasionally strike. There are so many fish in there that often times you can see two or three fish come take a look, sometimes racing over to beat the others. Clark caught two more fish, but with the wind making things difficult, particularly for me and my propensity towards tangles even in calm weather, we decided two hours of fishing here was enough.

After that we drove up the valley and found a picnic table sheltered by trees at a closed-for-the-season campground and ate the sandwiches we had brought with us. Once back at the house the women continued their visiting, Clark opted to relax and I headed back out to fish the river. I fished for about an hour and a half - this time protected from the wind by the steep banks - and caught a solitary fish, once again on the purple Prince Nymph.

Rejected

On the second weekend of November Kathy had plans in metro-Denver, so on short notice I invited my brother Dave up to the mountain house, as well as my friend Tucker and Todd, all of whom couldn't make it. Todd was recovering from recent rotator-cuff surgery on his right shoulder and rejected my suggestion that he fish with his left arm. But with a beautiful weather forecast of sunny and 50 degrees for both Saturday and Sunday, and mindful that this could be the last nice weekend for some time, I decided to drive up to Chaffee County by myself. I took my time getting to the river in order to give the water a chance to warm up, fishing from about 1 p.m. until it started getting dark around 4:45. By then my feet were numb from the cold water, despite the sunny skies and warm air temperature. I caught a brown and a rainbow, both around 11 inches, one on a purple Prince Nymph, and the other on a chironomid.

I was on the river by about 11 the following day, and got a vigorous strike on my very first cast, once again on the purple Prince Nymph. But I was standing on a boulder above the river and as I was climbing down to get to the water to net and release the fish it shook free. For two hours afterward I didn't have even a whiff of a strike, although the water seemed even more promising the further I worked my way upstream. I tried several different patterns before finally returning to the purple Prince Nymph, and I immediately caught an 11-inch brown. I concluded the weekend by fishing for another hour without any action, except for the excitement of losing a pair of reading glasses and breaking a zinger.

Suckmosis

Kathy hadn't been up to the mountain place for several weeks, so with decent weather expected until Sunday, we made the two-hour drive up to Chaffee County on a mid-December Friday morning. Earlier that week I had been fooling around with a little underwater video camera that I had purchased about four years ago when our granddaughter was born. I'm not sure why I purchased a waterproof camera, it's not like the birth was going to be underwater. Although the wedding was on a beach, 2000 miles from where we live in land-locked Colorado, so I guess it wouldn't have surprised me if the parents returned to give birth at the same spot.

The camera worked for a few months when it was new, but since then it has refused to hold a battery charge. Every once in a while I try to get the thing working again by using the main technical-repair skill I know: firmly smacking it. Occasionally I'll elevate the process when I'm particularly frustrated and knock it against something hard, or simply throw it down on the sidewalk and kick it across the street. Not surprisingly these efforts have all failed.

Apparently these particular name-brand cameras are real pieces of crap, because an online search found dozens of people with the exact same problem. And every person with a problem thinks they have a solution, typically involving technical stuff such as hydrofragging the sphincto-server core. Don't quote me verbatim on this advice, but to a non-techie like me that may as well be what they are saying. But one guy had what he swore was a simple solution, which was to simultaneously press and hold the on/off button while plugging the camera into the charger. This was about as complicated a maneuver as I could handle, so I gave it a try and damn if it didn't seem to work.

About a year ago, when I thought I had the camera working at that time, and inspired by my nephew A.J. and the cool videos he shoots on his GoPro camera, I decided to try some point-of-view videography. But I also tried to prove that I didn't need a fancy Go-Pro with all the proprietary chest-harnesses, head-mounts and sky-cams. So I grabbed my fishing cap, drilled a hole right through the brim, ran a ¼-20 bolt up through the bottom, threaded on a nut to hold it, then spun my piece of junk camera onto the remaining bolt threads. I then walked around the house looking like a total dork while trying to get some video footage. But of course the camera crapped out yet again, and I wound up with a ruined fishing cap.

But now, a year later, with the hole in my cap a constant reminder that my video camera sucks, I decided to try again since the camera seemed to be working. I inserted the bolt back through the hole in the hat bill, spun the camera on and placed the unwieldy rig on the dashboard of the truck for the short drive upriver. Once I pulled off the road I put the hat on, grabbed my gear and walked toward the river, the camera running for most of the five-minute walk. Once I was on the water, which had just a trace of ice around the rivers edge, I made sure the camera was on, and prepared for a strike on my first cast. And of course now that I was wearing this ridiculous-looking, homemade, redneck hat-cam, the fish wouldn't have anything to do with me.

The water was very clear so finally, after about an hour, I decided to switch out the fluorescent, football-shaped strike indicator for a white-yarn indicator, and almost immediately hooked a fish. And of course, just as I did, I heard the low-battery warning beep on the camera. Luckily the fish came to the net fairly quickly, and I was rewarded with a nice 12-inch brown that had eaten my upper fly, the purple Prince Nymph. When I reviewed the video footage later, the camera had indeed captured the hook-up, and recorded the short fight and a split-second of the fish in the net. There was not enough battery power to show the hero shot of me holding the fish, the fly removal, or the successful release of the fish.

Perhaps I was paying too much attention to capturing the whole thing on video and not enough to fishing, because after releasing the fish I wound up with a massive tangle just below the tippet knot. So I re-rigged with a black foam beetle sporting a stylish white parachute as my indicator, and was quite surprised when a fish hit that dry fly. I had it on the hook only long enough to see a 16-inch brown crash through the surface with an Olympic-caliber twisting-somersault maneuver while ejecting the fly. I fished for another hour without additional success before the sun went behind the mountain and it quickly got cold and dark.

I had a chance to review all the video footage over a cold beer back at the house. The shots of driving to the river were actually the best, the camera doing a good job of filming the snow-capped peaks set off by the clear, blue sky. Once I actually put the hat on though, things went downhill immediately. Instead of capturing the beauty of the surroundings as was my intention, I had a bunch of footage of my feet trudging through the sandy, rocky soil, across the abandoned railroad tracks and practically tumbling down the riverbank. It seems that the weight of the camera had pulled the bill of my cap down, angling the lens so it pointed down to my feet. The bright side is that if the boot manufacturer wants some footage of me walking to the river, and then standing in the water in my three-year-old boots, I'll have plenty to offer.

I'm not sure why, perhaps I finally got tired of my hat-bill covering my eyes and I pushed the hat back on my head, but somehow when I caught that fish, the camera actually captured the whole thing fairly decently. But of course, when I sat down at the computer to compile the little bit of useable footage, the editing software resisted all my attempts to actually edit. I believe I mentioned earlier that the camera sucks, but now I would like to go on record as saying the editing software also sucks. Big-time suckmosis majora.

YEAR 6

If You Give a Mouse a Front-End Loader

Math Whiz

Like last year, my first fishing-related outing of the new year would not find me on the river, but rather in an exhibit hall. Todd and I decided to go to the Fly Fishing Show this year instead of the Sportsman's Expo. It is a smaller event held at a smaller venue, but it is dedicated to fly fishing, so there were more fly fishing exhibitors there than at the larger, more diverse Sportsman's Expo. I was on a mission to find a good deal on new waders and boots. I have been envious of my son-in-law Bronson and the new boots he bought a year ago, particularly since they are tall and provide better ankle support and protection than my fairly low-cut boots. I have a tendency to slide off whatever slippery rock I happen to be fishing from or walking on, and slam my shins into the next rock. As a result I spend most of the year with black and blue bruises just above the top of my boots. Bruises that start to dissipate around December and finally disappear in March, just before the weather starts to warm up and it's time to start fishing again.

So new boots were a priority until my three-year old, $80 Costco waders began leaking. I'm not complaining about the durability, I figure my cost-per-outing with these waders was about $1. For more expensive name-brand waders to provide a similar value I would need to get about 500 fishing days out of them, which for me and my current rate of about 30 fishing days per year, would mean they would have to last almost 17 years. I am sure there is no way that even the best waders would last 17 years. 17 years from now the closest I'll probably get to a fish will be when someone is spoon-feeding me fish-flavored gruel at the local retirement home.

I spent so much time at the Fly Fishing Show shopping for waders and boots that there was no time left for the free classes, seminars and casting demonstrations. Thankfully there were factory reps there from the major manufacturers who were willing to spend plenty of time to make sure I spent my money on their equipment. I wound up getting an alleged 20 percent off what I consider to be the exorbitant retail price of the current-model boots I wanted, and 30 percent off discontinued waders that are supposedly "better than the new model that replaced them." But for these name-brand waders to provide the same value as my Costco waders, they will need to last over nine years. Hopefully nine years from now my mind won't be so far gone that I will still remember how to fish, if you can call what I do fishing. At my current rate of descent, I may be lucky just to remember my name by then.

Blown Away

It had been six weeks since we had been to the mountains, so with decent weather and dry roads predicted for the third weekend of January, Kathy and I decided we should go up and check on the place. We were pleasantly surprised to find no mice in the traps, nor any evidence of mice elsewhere. We were disappointed in the weather however. Even though it was fairly warm (for January) the wind blew strong and relentless all weekend, keeping us inside for the duration. We made the best of it by re-caulking the two master-bathroom sink cabinets and replacing the $5 light fixtures in the laundry room and hallway with marginally better $10 light fixtures. It was not exactly an action-packed weekend, but a necessary trip to insure there were no wild animals living in the house, or that the house hadn't blown away altogether.

Fairies and Fish

I am fortunate that my office for my day job is in my house. Sure, I miss the face-to-face interaction with actual, real-live people in the work world at times, but with the rise in electronic communication, those types of transactions in my field are no longer common. After my business partner (and father) passed away nine years ago, the only live interactions I was having was the occasional "Good morning" with someone in the elevator, or a nod and a mumbled "How's it going?" with the guy at the next urinal. Moving the office to the house was mostly a financial decision at the time. Why continue to pay thousands of dollars per year for rent when I could easily function just as well from home? When we bought our house a few years earlier, we knew this was a likely future scenario, so we bought a house that had a good room for a private office, away from the distractions of the rest of the house.

A benefit unforeseen at that time however, is the opportunity to spend quality time with my grandkids. Kathy watches granddaughter Haley (now 4) and Grandson Kaden (1), two days a week. And yes, getting up at 6 a.m. to shower, shave and dress prior to their 6:30 arrival can be difficult, particularly when it is dark, cold and sometimes snowing outside, until they come bouncing through the doorway with infectious ear-to-ear smiles. They often bring over other infectious surprises, but those inconveniences are also worth it considering the joy they bring to my life.

After lunch with Kathy and the kids today, I was absentmindedly flipping through a fly- gear catalog while I finished drinking a cup of hot tea. While Kaden banged out a tune on his high-chair tray, Haley waited impatiently for our usual after-lunch play time, which typically involves checking the "fairy jar" for little "fairy things" that the fairies, with my help, have left there for Haley to discover. It's cute to see her get so excited about anything fairy related, but after several months of this it has gotten a little tedious for me. It's a bit like perpetuating the Santa Claus myth every day of the year. So perhaps I was stalling just a little before chasing after unseen fairies. Haley decided to wait by climbing up onto my lap to see what I was reading. As I turned each page in the catalog, she asked very intelligent questions about the part each item played in fly fishing. She was also quite interested in the photos of people standing in beautiful rivers casting a fly line about, and of course the photos of those same people holding colorful rainbow, brook, brown and cutthroat trout.

When we got to the pages in the catalog that showed the flies, she became even more curious. At first she had a hard time believing that fish would be gullible enough to eat anything with a pointy hook attached. But I explained that fish often don't take the time to study the fly - that they'll suck it up quickly if it is the same size and color of, and is moving like, a natural insect. Once it is in their mouth however, they can tell that something isn't right and they will spit it out before they swallow it. But just before they spit it out is when the fly fisherman lifts the rod tip to set the hook firmly into the fishes lip, I explained, showing her the motion with an imaginary fly rod.

Her eyes got wide as she asked, "Then what happens?"

"Well, if you're lucky the fly will hook the fishes lip. Then you feel the fish on the end of your line, and its tugging and pulling and trying to get that hook out of its mouth."

"Does it hurt it?" she asked, concerned as always for the welfare of wild things.

"Well, I suppose it stings a little. Kind of like when you get a shot at the doctor."

"Oh," she said quietly. That's a pain that's fresh in the mind of a four-year old. "What happens next?"

"Well, the fish will start to swim away real fast, while still trying to get that hook out of its lip. It will shake its head from side to side, and sometimes it will jump out of the water, twisting and spinning and spraying water everywhere."

"What do *you* do?"

"I'm trying to keep that fish on the line by keeping the line tight. You do that by pulling in any extra line and keeping your rod tip pointed up or away from the fish. If you do everything right, eventually the fish will get tired and you can reel it in and guide it into your net."

"Then you take the fly out of the fishes mouth?" she asked.

"That's right. First you get your hands wet, because that's better for the fish. Then you put your hand around it gently to hold it and you take your little scissors and pull the fly right out of its lip."

"And then you let it go?"

"Yes, and it swims back so it can be with its family."

She looked thoughtfully back at the photos of the small flies and then asked "Can I see *your* flies?"

"Sure you can, honey." I led her to the closet that holds my fishing gear, and pulled out my fly boxes. I showed her my midge and nymph box first.

"They're so tiny. Can I touch them?" she asked.

"Yes, but be real careful, OK? Remember they have hooks in them," I cautioned.

She began to softly stroke the flies, like she was petting very tiny kittens. "Where are the hooks?" she asked.

"The hooks are on the bottom, stuck into the foam." I pulled out my dry fly box and let her gently rub those flies, explaining the difference between dry flies and nymphs. And then I showed her the streamers, which led her to ask about why some of them had eyes. I explained that the eyes helped them look like baby fish, which I immediately regretted.

"Fish eat their babies?" she asked in shock.

"Well, um, err, not their *own* babies. But sometimes they might try to eat other little fish. Like in the movie 'Finding Nemo.'" *Whew.*

"Oh. Can I see your rod?" she suddenly asked. I was proud that she was getting the terminology down and didn't call it a pole.

I opened the rod case and showed her the rod, and after she looked it over she asked to see my net. I removed the net from my gear bag and she expressed surprise at how big it was. I elected not to tell her the whole story about how I ordered it online and that I was also surprised at how big it was when it was delivered.

"Papa?" she asked. "Will you take me fishing?"

"I would love to take you fishing. We'll go this summer, OK?"

"Yes! I can hardly wait!"

She skipped off to look for fairies, while I happily put the gear away, thankful that working from the house makes these kinds of moments possible.

Stayin' Alive, Stayin' Alive...ah, ha, ha, ha

The first Saturday in February was sunny, calm and unseasonably warm in Denver, so I decided to try to patch my old, leaky waders for use as a spare pair. I had watched a couple of videos online where people turned their waders inside out and filled them with water, then sat back and watched as the holes made themselves evident by shooting out streams of water. I started by laying the inside-out waders on a clean tarp that I had placed on the winter-grunged deck, sticking a garden hose down one leg and then turning on the hose. I realized the error of my ways as soon as the water started running out the chest opening, and not before. Water of course seeks its own level and I just had the waders flat out on the deck, now sitting in a puddle of water.

After I let the inside (now the outside) dry, I took the waders next door to my friend Jack's house, whose deck has a railing around the perimeter. I laid the waders over the railing and secured the suspenders, which were laying on the deck surface, by placing a large rock on them. As I filled them with water I was able to wrestle the waders around enough to mark several leaky spots. But more troubling than that was all the water that appeared to be leaking through the seams. I had marked several suspicious spots when suddenly the weight of the water-filled waders caused the suspenders to slice right through my anchor rock, breaking it in half! The waders immediately plummeted to the ground, soaking me in a geyser of smelly wader water. I dropped the hose, which started dancing like John Travolta, resulting in me jumping around spastically to avoid the cold spray while trying not to trip over the sack-of-shit waders now flaccid at my feet. *Well this isn't working out how I imagined.* That's about the time I realized that in each wader-repair video I watched there were two people involved in the process: one to work the hose and mark the leaks, the other to handle the heavy, water-filled waders. Dripping wet, I rolled up the hose and threw the waders in the trash.

Ground Control to Major Todd

With unusually nice weather expected for mid-February, and with the fly shop predicting good fishing on the Arkansas, I asked Todd if his surgically-repaired shoulder was ready for fishing. Todd said his physical therapist had just recently suggested he get out and put his shoulder to the test, so after a few phone calls and text messages, Todd said yes he could get away to fish this weekend. He said that Laurie could come also and that the two of them would stay at their Chaffee County place. And Kathy decided that since Laurie was coming she would too. But Todd soon learned from others in his mountain home-ownership group that some water pipes had burst recently, rendering their place without water until a plumber could make the necessary repairs. So Laurie and Todd and their little dog Snowball stayed at our place. We met there around noon on Saturday, Laurie and Todd driving separate because Todd thought it could be necessary to leave early due to some health concerns of a family member. It was all kind of complicated for little more than a 24-hour stay, but the unbelievable weather made it worthwhile.

After a sandwich, Todd and I headed to an area along the river that we thought would have sun on the water and therefore bug and trout activity. The car thermometer read 61 degrees and there was not the slightest suggestion of wind – almost unheard of for this time of year. But before we got to where we were planning to fish we saw a previously unnoticed and apparently new public fishing access. We pulled off the highway to take a look and found a tiny parking area–room for four cars at most. There was a huge sign there, undoubtedly readable from outer space, listing confusing regulations about which areas could be fished and how. We decided to check it out anyway, so we pulled on our waders and boots and got our gear together. I reached into the car for my rod and reel and was dismayed to find that I had neglected to bring them along. I was glad to make this discovery fairly close to the house and not at our originally intended destination another 20 minutes down the road.

Todd left to scout the river and I drove his car back to the house to retrieve my rod. Laurie was glad to see me because her hiking boots were in the car and she and Kathy were getting ready to hike. After the 20-minute delay I followed the access trail from the little parking lot, which led directly to an old railing-free railroad bridge that crossed high above the river, on which Todd now stood. We looked down at the river and tried to figure out where we were allowed to fish, standing as close to edge of the bridge as we dared. It seems a giant international bottled-water company, in exchange for sucking billions of gallons of spring water from the valley aquifer, had to allow fishing along six acres of river that bordered their spring site. Apparently this deal didn't actually specify that they had to make clear to the public which six acres, which side of the river and upstream or downstream of the bridge.

We decided that the east bank, south of the bridge looked the best for fly fishing this day, so lacking any lucid guidance regarding restrictions, we continued across the bridge then down through the thickets to get to the river. We didn't see any "No Trespassing" signs, so we tied on our flies - an attractor nymph followed by a small midge for me - and worked our way along the river for about a half mile. We both tried several different flies but nothing was working, the water apparently still too cold. We decided to drive to another spot along the river so we worked our way back toward the bridge, still casting into the most promising water as we came upon it, and still without success.

We wound up fishing closer to the house, where our luck was the same, so as the sun went down around 5:30 we packed it in and headed out (rawhide). But neither of us were too discouraged: it was a beautiful, calm, sunny day and we were fishing clear water with awesome views of snow-capped 14,000 foot mountains. I am also happy to report that my brand-new waders and boots performed up to my lofty expectations on their maiden voyage, keeping me warm, dry and solidly planted in the very cold water of the Arkansas River.

Back at the house we were greeted by the mouth-watering aroma of buffalo pot roast simmering in the crock pot. We learned that Kathy and Laurie had walked out of the front door and hiked up and around the nearby hillside for three hours, immensely enjoying the unseasonably warm weather. The following day the weather was back to normal, a fast-moving storm dumping abundant snow along our route home, resulting in a flurry of accidents and snarled traffic.

Mr. Joe Tangles

After several weeks of miserable winter weather, this mid-March weekend looked very promising: sunny and warm. Unfortunately Kathy was getting over a nasty flu bug, and since I didn't catch it we assumed it was the same strain that sidelined me between Christmas and New Years. The only upside to that illness was that between trips to the bathroom I became an expert on The Rifleman TV show while camped on the couch. Yet another skill to add to my résumé. So Kathy took one last day to recover and we drove up to Chaffee County on Sunday morning. I wasn't really planning to rush out and fish as soon as we got there, but that's pretty much what happened. At least it felt like I was rushing. The warm, sunny, calm day was practically begging me to fish and I was anxious to comply. But by the time we had lunch and I got geared up it was 2 p.m. before I made my first cast.

It seems like the bigger the rush I'm in the more spastic I become. I forget important pieces of gear and spend precious time rounding up everything. It takes me longer to tie on tippet and flies because my knots keep failing. I have trouble reaching around behind me to secure my net. I batten down my waders with my car keys still in hand and have to unbatten, secure the keys in my pants beneath the waders, and rebatten. But when I got to the river, and saw the trout lined up and feeding in a deep, clear pool I immediately began to relax. My casts were accurate and had good distance when I needed. But despite this, and the fact that I thought I was being stealthy, the trout refused my offering, even after trying different flies, more weight and more depth. It didn't take me long to get frustrated. *Come on, you stupid fish.*

I finally moved upstream and away from that pool and immediately began a pattern that persisted for the rest of the day: tangles. If Jerry Jeff Walker wrote a song about me he would call it Mr. Joe Tangles.

I knew a spaz Joe Tangles and he'd fish for you
In brand new boots
With little hair and skinny legs and crappy vision
And a scrawny caboose

He fished like crap
Fished like crap
And tried not to fall in

(Everybody!)
Mr. Joe Tangles
Mr. Joe Tangles
Mr. Joe Tangles
...Fish

I doubt it would be recorded by as many artists as Jerry Jeff's masterpiece *Mr. Bojangles*: at least 50 at last count including of course Mr. Walker himself and The Nitty Gritty Dirt Band, but also such luminaries as Bob Dylan, Garth Brooks, Elton John, Neil Diamond and Sammy Davis Jr. And for some reason William Shatner, Homer Simpson and the actress that played Lilith on "Cheers". No offense to Shatner and Lilith, but of the last three, I think I'd rather listen to Homer sing it.

Anyway for the next 3-1/2 hours I got snagged on bushes and trees, and every time I pulled my line out of the water to inspect it, it was wrapped around my flies, indicator and weight like a burrito on the gas station floor. I spent four times longer untangling these messes than I did actually fishing. It was like I had accidently set my fly rod to "Massive Tangle" mode. Finally, at about 6 p.m. I had a hit. But all I got after setting the hook was a few tugs in reply and then nothing. I reeled in to check my line and was greeted with another massive tangle. This one bore an uncanny resemblance to Art Garfunkel's afro. I wonder if Art Garfunkel ever sang Mr. Bojangles.

Don't Mess with Bacon

Monday was another beautiful day, but I was so discouraged from Sunday's outing that I didn't want to go anywhere near my fly rod. I figured if I even looked in its direction the line would immediately tangle on the reel. Instead I replaced the piece-of-junk kitchen faucet with a slightly better kitchen faucet. Like most projects, it took twice as long as it should have when I also had to replace the leaky supply lines. After an early lunch Kathy and I took a walk along the river, stopping occasionally to try and spot fish, but without success.

When we got back to the house I was tempted to return to the river with my fly rod, but by then my stomach was feeling gnarly like it had the previous night. We had gone out to dinner and I had one of my favorites: a salmon sandwich topped with bacon. But for some reason the restaurant decided they could improve on the flavor of the delicious-all-by-itself bacon by coating it with a thick layer of spicy pepper. And for some reason I ate it like that, much to my discomfort. So instead of trying to redeem myself for yesterday's abysmal fishing effort, I decided to take a nap. Because as I like to say, there's no problem that can't be solved by a nap.

Boom Boom Boom Boom

Our next trip to the cabin came on the last Friday in March, and shortly after pulling in we walked a couple hundred yards to the river. Conveniently, I happened to be wearing my waders and carrying my fly rod. When we reached the small parking area at the river there was a younger guy gearing up for spin fishing at his car with his stereo blasting hip-hop music so loud that I could actually see pebbles and dirt clods bouncing up from the ground in rhythm. I feared the boom-boom bass would vibrate sonic waves through the water and send the fish scurrying downriver to the Gulf of Mexico, which is where I wanted to go when I heard it. There's nothing like a little urban music at roughly the sound level of a DC-10 at takeoff to get you in touch with nature.

Kathy continued her walk along the path that parallels the river and I headed down to the water. But after I climbed halfway down the bank I saw a young couple through the trees, rigging up their spinning rods right where I was planning to enter the water. So I climbed back up the bank and walked upstream to another spot. But as I was getting ready to venture down the bank to the water I saw that the same couple had now moved upstream to the same spot. So I walked *back* downstream to where I was originally going to start, sat on a rock and tied on a couple of nymphs. The boom-boom music guy showed up, but he walked upstream to join the other two. They fished from a large boulder and into a nice pool for about 45 minutes, while I fished downstream from them. They finally got bored and left and I headed upstream, covering a fair amount of water for the next hour or so.

After awhile a father and young son appeared on the riverbank, just sort of hanging around. The son, maybe six-years-old, said to me, "There's no fish in here you know."

"Yes, there are," I replied.

"No there aren't."

"*Yes*, there are."

"*No*, there aren't."

"OK," I finally gave in, deciding to be the mature one for once. And maybe he was right, because I didn't even have a nibble, much less catch a fish. Kid 1, Old Guy 0.

Life's Been Good

With another summer approaching, and the onset of carpet-beetle weather, we were determined once again to get a handle on our little problem. After breakfast on Saturday we gathered up some tools and headed for the bug room. This bedroom has bold purple paint and used to have vivid purple carpet before we ripped it out in frustration a year and a half ago. So now it's just a bare plywood subfloor that Kathy painted white, which helps us to see the tiny black bugs and the tinier tan-colored larvae. The lower half of the walls in this room are covered in wainscot and poorly trimmed in the same plastic fake-wood that infects much of the rest of the house.

After a fair amount of discussion, we decided to pull a piece of wainscot off the wall to see what was behind it. Hopefully a big beetle nest that we could destroy and be done with the years-old problem in one fell-swoop. To get the wainscot panel off the wall we had to remove some of the cheesy plastic trim, which of course broke into 400 little pieces in the process. And for some reason the wainscot panel was attached to the wall with 18,216 nails, but amazingly we were able to remove it relatively intact. What we found behind it was disappointing. Not the center of the carpet beetle universe like we had hoped, but rather a couple of dozen dead beetles clinging to the drywall. *Crap.* I guess the next step is to remove a hunk of drywall and see if we find anything behind *it*.

By then it had warmed up sufficiently from the 20 degrees of first light for us to take our usual two-mile walk along the river. By the time we returned it was lunch time, and after lunch it was fishing time. I chose a spot where I could cast upstream with my right arm toward the river. This simplifies things for me immensely because I don't get snagged on streamside vegetation nearly as often. Don't get me wrong, I still hook into the occasional cottonwood tree, just not as often as I do from the opposite bank.

After parking the car I walked to the river and searched for a way down the steep, rocky, slope that hopefully wouldn't cause a broken leg or a rip in my new waders. Once I found a likely path I climbed down only to find another fly fisherman. This is the second day in a row that someone has been at the spot I was planning to fish, after it only happening to me twice in the last several years. Come to think of it those previous two times were on the same day. So I climbed back up the bank and debated as to whether I should head upstream or down. I generally fish pretty slowly, methodically covering the water. Of course all those tangles and snags I get do little to speed me along. I walked downstream, figuring the chances of me overtaking the other guy were much slimmer than him passing me.

I started off fishing a nice-looking, medium-depth pool that was being warmed by the sun. I used a Prince of Darkness nymph as my top fly and a small, olive RS2 dangling 16 to 20 inches below that. On my third cast I saw the indicator unmistakably dip and did everything right in order to pull in a little brown that had decided the Prince of Darkness looked appetizing. My first fish of the year! I estimated it to be about nine inches before I remembered the new tape-measure zinger I had bought over the winter to replace the normal zinger that had broken late last season. My forceps were attached to this new zinger, so when I pulled them out to remove the hook I took the opportunity to measure the fish. It didn't cooperate by lying straight and still, instead curling its tail around while I struggled to maintain control of my rod, my net, the fish and the tape measure. But despite all this I was able to determine that it was at least 10-1/2 inches long.

A few casts later I pulled another brownie out of this same pool, who had also hit the Prince Nymph. This one played it smart by trying to bury itself down deep among the large rocks, and I had to work to keep it from getting there without breaking free. Once in the net I estimated it to be 10 inches, but the tape-measure zinger proved me wrong again when it showed 12 inches. Unlike many anglers, I guess I have a tendency to underestimate the size of the fish I catch. Maybe I should use this zinger to get an accurate measurement of my ... umm ... errr ... never mind.

I considered removing the RS2 and just fish with the successful Prince Nymph, but then thought better of messing with a fruitful set-up. After that first pool played out I moved up to another promising spot, this one closer to the main channel of the river. But before I splashed my way through a shallow riffle to get there I threw a few flies in just to make sure there were no fish in the riffle. And wouldn't you know it, a strike in no more than eight inches of water, and on the RS2.

After catching three fish in the first half hour, I didn't catch another for an hour. After that fourth fish another hour went by before catching my final fish of the day, although I did have an unlanded strike in-between. All told, I fished for 3-1/2 hours and caught five brown trout. Better fishermen than me would have no doubt caught many more, but I was thrilled. A warm, sunny, calm, early-spring day spent fly fishing for trout in the Colorado Rocky Mountains. Life doesn't get much better.

Breakfast Activity

We were planning to hike on Sunday morning but the velocity of the wind would have made for an uncomfortable trek. So we went out for breakfast instead because as I like to say, "When it's windy, go to breakfast." I've also been known to go to breakfast when it's not windy. Really any excuse to go out for breakfast is fine with me. Unless it's something like falling off the roof and breaking my back, in which case I would probably elect *not* to go out for breakfast. When we got back from breakfast, lo and behold, the wind had calmed down substantially and the weather was just about perfect for a late March hike. Kathy said it would be fine with her if I would rather fish, but I declined, saying I wanted to spend time with her. Aren't I sweet? Besides, I didn't want to spoil the warm glow I had from yesterday's outing by possibly coming up empty today.

Has Old Pete Gone Berserk?

Another nice weekend was anticipated in mid-April so we drove up to Chaffee County on Friday afternoon, pulling in around 4 p.m. We would have made it there a little earlier, but for much of the trip we had a sheriff's vehicle right behind us. He finally passed us but then stayed right in front of us, and I didn't really think it prudent to blow past him. Although it was sunny, there was a cold breeze blowing so I elected not to fish, instead just hanging around and enjoying the mountain house.

On Saturday morning we had a plumber come over to take a look at the water pressure in one of the showers. This guy was recommended to us by Laurie and Todd - they had numerous water pipes burst over the winter that resulted in several thousand dollars in damage. I am hopeful that our bill will be substantially less. He worked diligently for an hour or so before deciding we needed a new valve, which of course is a type that is no longer made. The bottom line is that we won't know the bottom line until he can locate a valve, replace it and see if it works.

Once the plumber left Kathy and I went for a stroll along the river, the day a little breezy, but sunny and warming nicely. While we were walking Todd texted me to say that he and Laurie were at their river house, and asked if I wanted to go up and fish. Their place is eight miles north of ours and several hundred feet higher in elevation than where I do much of my fishing. As I understand it, this difference in elevation has an impact on the water temperature and therefore the insect and fish activity. In the springtime, the water warms first at lower elevations and is typically a more desirable place to fish. In the heat of the summer however, the trout are more lethargic, conserving their energy in the warmer, lower elevation water. Fishing cooler, higher elevation water can be more productive come July and August. I had what I considered a pretty successful day two weeks ago at one of my usual spots and was anxious to repeat it. But I also had to weigh the advantage of hanging-out with Todd and fishing his less-fished, but cooler private water. I accepted his invitation and after lunch I drove upstream to Todd and Laurie's place.

They were in spring-cleaning mode when I got there, made more urgent by the broken-water-pipe mess. Laurie was scurrying around wearing her ubiquitous rubber cleaning-gloves and Todd was wearing his fishing waders while moving boxes that were filled with mushy belongings. I'm not sure if he was wearing his waders to protect his clothes from the soggy chore, or if he was getting a head-start on fishing. In any event, by the time I was geared up he was also ready to go, both of us finally stepping into the river close to 2 p.m. I started with the successful combination of two weeks earlier - a Prince of Darkness followed by an RS2, thinking perhaps this water was at the same stage as the downstream water of fourteen days earlier - but was disappointed when I didn't hook a fish right away. Todd caught a brown trout within 15 minutes on a fly that looked like a small Pheasant Tail, only with a pink bead-head that was intended to resemble a small egg. I have no idea what you call the thing - perhaps an Egg-Sucking Pheasant Tail?

I stuck with my flies as we approached water that usually yields fish – a spot where the river reunites after separating around a small island. I was rewarded 10 minutes later with a beautiful 14-inch rainbow in spawning colors that hit the Prince Nymph. Todd waded over from mid-river to where I stood near the west shore so he could take a photo. Once he reviewed the picture he admonished me for the way I held the fish: both hands wrapped around it hiding half the fish. I explained that being the spaz that I am, I have a hard time holding on to the slimy suckers. Todd said the key was to gently secure the tail. Unfortunately I didn't get much of an opportunity to practice this technique the rest of the afternoon.

I did hook into another fish several minutes later and for a few moments the fish acted as if it didn't know that it had been caught. Once it did, however, it put up a heck of a fight. That thing swam around for almost 10 minutes while I tried not to tire it out too much, but without letting it off. When it finally allowed itself to be netted, I saw what the deal was: I had foul-hooked it in the dorsal fin. Oops. After some revival it swam off to reclaim its place among its upstream-facing compatriots, leaving me with a nicely tangled line.

I took the opportunity to tie on a new set of nymphs, this time an egg-pattern up top and a small, purple Psycho Nymph below that. I casted this combination in the same productive water a few times but moved up when it didn't elicit a strike. I waded along the west shore of the west channel, an area with cut-banks that I had always been anxious to try but shied away from due to the low-hanging vegetation. But the spring runoff had not yet begun and the water level was still relatively low, so there was a larger margin for error than there would be later in the season. I casted along the cut-bank several times before finally getting my flies in a nice drift beneath the overhanging shore. My indicator dipped, I set the hook and wham, big resistance. The fish immediately ran for the center of the channel and then took a serpentine route downstream. This was a big, fast-swimming fish that was 25 yards downstream before I knew what the hell was happening. When I came to my senses I realized it was bolting for some large rocks and I was afraid it would lodge beneath them. But when I tried to guide the fish away from the rocks my line suddenly went slack. *Damn!*

Undeterred, I continued wading upstream, casting along the shoreline until I got snagged on some rocks just above the waterline. Not wanting to spook any fish that may be lurking, I gave the line a jerk to free my flies instead of splashing my way through the lane, but of course my tippet knot broke. Deterred, I splashed through the lane anyway to retrieve my flies and indicator but when I got there they were nowhere to be found. The water for the next quarter mile ahead didn't look nearly as inviting, but I sat down along the bank and tied on a new rig anyway. When I was finished I looked around again for my missing flies and indicator and saw instead an intact deer ribcage and various other bones scattered around right where I had been sitting.

I continued upstream toward a promising place where I have caught fish before: a spot where a headgate brings warmer irrigation water back into the river. The river in between is wide, shallow and featureless, but I continued throwing in flies anyway as I made my way to the good spot. At least it was easy wading. 20 yards below my destination, Todd whistled to me from across the river. I looked over to see him motioning to me in a low-key, subdued manner. I couldn't tell what he was trying to tell me so I kept fishing. 10 yards before reaching the honey-hole he whistled again. I looked over and again he was making cryptic hand signals that I didn't understand. "What?" I called. He whisper-shouted something I couldn't hear over the sound of the water cascading into the river from the irrigation ditch.

"WHAT?" I yelled louder.

"Steve!" Todd said, pointing at something or someone over my shoulder.

"WHO THE HELL IS STEVE?" I yelled back.

Exasperated, Todd called, "Old Pete!"

Oh, so his name is Steve. I always called him Old Pete, because, well, he's old, I could never remember his name, and he just looked like a Pete.

"SO?" I yelled.

Todd gave me the slashing-throat signal and motioned me over to his side of the river. I knew I was technically fishing Old Pete's water, but I thought Todd had an arrangement with him. Why would Todd want me to wade out of Pete's water? I gave him the two palms up gesture, universal language for *what the hell*?

"Wade downstream and then come across as soon as you can," Todd whisper-shouted. "And keep low."

Now I was a little alarmed. *Keep low?* Had Old Pete gone berserk and was now heading my way with a shotgun? I waded downstream as quickly and nonchalantly as possible, while at the same time trying to make myself a smaller target.

Todd walked downstream to meet me, and once I had crossed over to the "safe" side of the river I said, "I thought you had permission to fish his water."

"I have to call him and ask each time, and I forgot to call."

"Oh, well, OK, thanks, I guess," I mumbled, thankful that Old Pete probably had never intended to blow me out of the water, but a little disappointed I wasn't able to fish his honey-hole.

Todd had to get back to his house to help Laurie with the spring cleaning, so he climbed out of the river to walk back. I tied on a streamer and fished my way back downstream without any interest from our friends the trout. Tally for the day: one legitimate catch, one foul-hooker and two that got off before I got them to the net. A little disappointing, but better than being inside on this beautiful spring day.

I Can't Get No...

We decided to hike the Midland Trail the next day and invited Laurie to join us. She accepted, but we were surprised when she said Todd would be coming too. We assumed that he would elect to fish instead. The Midland Trail follows the grade of the old railroad that ran to and from the valley until 1922. It is a relatively low elevation hike at around 8400 ft., so it's a good one between October and June when the higher elevation trails are inaccessible due to snow. In the summer months it can get surprisingly hot hiking around the sandy, mostly shadeless terrain. Kathy and I had hiked here about 2-1/2 years earlier in November and remembered it to be a pleasant stroll with awesome views of the snow-capped peaks across the valley. It's not much of a workout, even for us, as the elevation gain is so slight as to be almost unnoticeable. It is a popular trail for mountain bikers and people running with their dogs.

Just after we got started, a woman jogged past us going the opposite direction with two dogs, the larger dog proudly carrying the whole fur-covered, articulated leg of a deer, complete with the hoof. We hiked east from the trailhead for about two miles, admiring the views and enjoying the conversation, before deciding to stop for lunch. The day was a little windy, so we sought a spot to eat our sandwiches that was out of the wind, but still offered good views.

After lunch Todd suggested that perhaps this would be a good spot to turn around, I imagine so he could spend the afternoon fishing. No one objected, so we headed back the way we came. Todd and I got into a conversation about goose hunting, which led to a discussion about the various ways to kill a goose if the dog brings it back while still alive. Laurie finally put an end to the subject when I suggested that one guy could hold the goose's head while another held the feet, and a third guy could back the truck over its neck. (I was of course just joking here, in a big brother grossing-out-his-sister way. I would never do this, nor would I condone this type of behavior. So please step away from the phone and resist the urge to call PETA.)

When we were less than a half mile from the end of the hike I stopped to tie my shoelaces, which I must do often for some reason. It probably has something to do with my ridiculously bony ankles not fitting well in the ankle-hole of my shoes. Anyway, after I was done tying my shoes for the third time that hour, I noticed a patch of fresh deer hide, perhaps 14 inches x 26 inches, draped over a tree branch about eight feet above the ground. While we all stood looking at it and wondering how it got there, I couldn't resist standing behind Laurie and whispering, "It sure is creepy," right before suddenly grabbing her arms. To my amusement she almost jumped out of her skin, but to her credit she didn't scream. Laurie has maintained for years that I tormented her when we were kids, which of course I didn't. But I figured as long as I was going to be blamed for it, I may as well actually get the satisfaction of it just this once.

A Tale of Two Half-Days

Kathy was out of state visiting family at the end of April, so I decided this would be a good time for a guy's weekend at the mountain place. Todd was available, but when I invited my brother Dave he said he didn't want to slow down our fishing. Dave's not heavily into fly-fishing like me and Todd, but I explained that this weekend wouldn't be all about fly fishing. Just three guys hanging out in the Colorado Rockies. When I told Todd that Dave had elected to take a rain-check, Todd said that he would call Dave and try to talk him into coming. Later, Dave played the voice mail for me that Todd had left on his phone.

Hello. If this is not Dave Curtin, please hang up immediately. But if this is Dave Curtin, please listen carefully to a fantastic offer. Dave Curtin, you've been chosen for an all-expenses-paid weekend trip to beautiful Chaffee County Colorado to go fly fishing with two expert – make that one expert - fly fisherman named Todd Walker. Your brother Chris Curtin will also be attending. Dave Curtin, if you choose to accept this wonderful gift: an all expenses paid trip to beautiful Chaffee County this coming weekend, please reply by calling now! Operators are standing by.

Dave did not accept the fantastic offer/wonderful gift, and my friend Tucker said he couldn't make it either, so once again it was just Todd and I for a weekend that turned out to be all about fly fishing after all.

Todd had a commitment on Friday evening so he wanted to leave for the mountains on Saturday at 7 a.m. I had no desire to get up at 6 on a Saturday, plus I wanted to take the truck and leave it for the season, so I drove up Friday afternoon. My plan was to fish Friday afternoon, but when I arrived there were snow flurries, which was no big deal, but the cold wind that was blowing *was* a big deal. So instead of fishing I got my gear together and generally prepared for Saturday morning so I could sleep as late as possible. Of course I woke at 6 a.m. anyway.

Todd pulled into the drive around 9:00 on the dull, gray morning and after he got organized we were on the river by 10:00. By 10:01 I had the first of many "how-the-hell-did-that-happen?" tangles that would bedevil me for the entire morning. Almost every time I pulled my line out of the water to inspect it I found the bottom fly caught up in the strike indicator. I also managed to wrap the leader around my rod several times, and I lost countless split shots by getting them wedged between rocks. I have been fly fishing semi-seriously and fairly regularly, averaging 30 days per year, for over three years now. You would think I would be able to cast a fly occasionally without forming a pickup-truck-sized tangle. I guess my erratic casting motion is just not conducive to problem-free fly fishing. If you look up the word "herky-jerky" in an old-fashioned, paper and ink dictionary, there is a little line-drawing of me fly fishing.

And so the morning continued, constant tangles and snags as I fished with two nymphs, split shot, putty weight and an indicator. This was perhaps the most frustrating time I've ever had fly fishing. I guess all that crap on the line is just too much for my lousy technique. We were fishing a section of the river that we had previously thought was privately owned, but now had reason to believe was public. After about three hours we decided to fish elsewhere, and I used the change of location as motivation to refresh my outlook. I always expect that I will have a good day of fishing, but once things start going south I have difficulty recovering.

We drove upstream about two miles, and my plan was to fish a Blue-Wing-Olive dry, which were beginning to hatch, with a BWO emerger below that. But once I tied on the dry fly, I decided to just go with that, telling myself *keep it simple, stupid*. Plus Todd caught a fish on a BWO dry while I was still dinkin' around at the truck and I was anxious to get in the river and change my luck. Mercifully my luck did change. Not that I caught a fish, although I did watch a little guy follow my fly downstream for several seconds, sip the fly and then spit it out, all without me setting the hook. It was only about five inches long, so I decided to save it the trauma. But casting the single fly seemed to be the ticket in getting my mojo back - if I ever had any mojo to begin with. We fished here for perhaps 45 minutes and I did not get a single tangle or snag, which had a positive effect in restoring my attitude.

We drove back downstream perhaps four miles, this time to a spot requiring a short trek through the piñons to reach the river. With my newly restored confidence I tied on a big, buoyant, easily seen hopper pattern and a Barr's Emerger below that. Within 15 minutes I caught a skinny, 12-inch brown on the emerger. 30 minutes went by without another strike, so I replaced the emerger with a small Golden Stone nymph and caught another brown, this one a little larger at 13 inches and not quite as thin as the first. 15 minutes later, as my hopper drifted passed a rock, I was taken by surprise by a sudden, splashy rise. Not really expecting any action on the hopper I was of course late in setting the hook. But a few minutes later I was ready when it happened again, catching my first fish on a dry fly of the year.

Unfortunately I lost that hopper, the only one of its kind that I had, along with the Golden Stone, when I got snagged on something below the surface in deep water. Since I couldn't wade out to retrieve it I had to take my chances with the old give-it-a-yank routine and of course my tippet knot broke. About that time a blustery wind came up, followed shortly by my cell phone ringing. I was at a critical point in trying to tie on a different foam hopper and another Golden Stonefly in the wind, so I couldn't get to my phone - sequestered in its sandwich bag in my zipped-shut chest pocket - before it stopped ringing. After I had the flies secured on the line I checked caller ID to see that it was Todd who had called from somewhere out of sight upriver, so I called him back.

"This wind is miserable. Do you want to go get something to eat and maybe come back out later?" he suggested. It was almost 5 p.m. and we hadn't had any lunch, just a little beef jerky. But I knew that after a hot meal and perhaps a beer I wouldn't be particularly motivated to return to the cold river. Besides, I was finally catching fish.

"I'm finally catching fish, Todd," I told him.

"Oh, great. Well, let's keep fishing then."

If I was thinking squarely I would have met up with Todd, tossed him the truck keys and suggested he go get something to eat and pick me up when he was done. But fly fishing does about the same thing to me as a middle-aged man that cute girls did to me as a teenager: messes with my ability to think straight. And yet now with fishing, as then with cute girls, I continue to seek out these crooked-thinking situations.

Thankfully the cold wind died down, but so did the bite. I replaced the golden-stone nymph with a little sparkly, multi-colored, emerger-nymph thing that I obviously don't know the name of. The sun finally appeared from behind the dark clouds to beam golden afternoon light through the trees and onto the water. It made for a tranquil setting, but forced me to be aware of my shadow on the river surface and the affect it may have on the fish below.

I worked my way upstream to an area where the river became wider and shallower, a place I had never fished before. I enjoyed fishing here because of the easy wading and the ability to reach more of the water. I always appreciate new stretches of river, and the warm sun after a long, gray day was icing on the cake.

In looking around for good lanes to drift my flies, I saw a couple of guys fishing the opposite bank. These were the first fishermen I had seen all day other than Todd. I am always self-conscious around other fishermen due to my crappy technique (see herky-jerky above), but when I caught a nice, jumping brown trout on the multi-colored emerger as the guys looked on, I did a mid-river victory dance and shouted across the river, "In your face, mo-fos!" Not really. I was as casual and nonchalant as I could be in landing and releasing the fish, like it was something I did every five minutes of my life. But catching that brown as they watched helped me feel less embarrassed about my spastic casting. Who knows, maybe they'll emulate my erratic style since I didn't see them catch any fish with their fancy, smooth-as-silk casts.

I continued upstream without any action until I slowly lifted my rod at the end of a long drift for another cast. This apparently was all that was needed to entice a strike. Another acrobatic brown had fallen for the old fake-bug trick, and it was none too interested in coming quietly to the net, jumping and running several times before finally allowing itself to be captured.

I'm not sure why, but it seems like after each fish caught recently, my leader has been twisted around into an aggravating knot. Todd thinks it could have to do with how I handle the rod while netting and releasing the fish. In other words, *pay attention to what you're doing, Spaz.*

As I was dealing with the tangle that resulted from this last catch, I was startled by a nearby voice inquiring, "How's it going?" I looked up to see an official-looking, uniform-clad, ranger dude standing on the riverbank. He asked to see my license and even though I always keep it in the same pocket in my chest-pack, I had a hard time finding it among the packets of leader and other similarly sized crap that I have in there. I finally pulled it out just as I was starting to worry that it had fallen out somewhere. I began wading toward the shore to show it to him, but after I had gone 30 feet or so, he said, "Just hold it up, I can see it from here." I wasn't sure whether to be miffed that he said that after I had waded 30 feet out of my way, or appreciate that I didn't need to wade another 20 feet to reach the shore. Once he saw my slow, wobbly wading he either took pity on me, or ran out of patience waiting for me to get there. In any event, he had kind of a hard time seeing what he was looking for on the license, which of course was the year, as he squinted through the gathering twilight.

"I thought I saw some other guys fishing nearby."

"They left once they realized I was catching all the fish," I joked.

"Are you releasing everything you catch?" he asked, not amused.

"Yes."

Once he was satisfied that I was legal, he disappeared back to wherever he had materialized from, and I looked upriver to try and spot Todd. I was now officially hungry, and my "lasts-up-to-5-hours" toe warmers were no longer effective now that they were on their eighth hour. I telephoned Todd but got no answer, so I left a message and followed up with a text, letting him know I was ready to quit for the day. With no response I quickened my pace upriver, casting into a few promising spots along the way. Eventually I saw Todd making his way downriver, so I assumed he had gotten my message and was ready to leave. I saw no reason to continue wading upriver, so I waited for him by continuing to fish. But when he saw me stopping to fish, he stopped and fished. I finally reeled my line in, walked upriver to where he was and said, "I'm ready whenever you are."

Thus ended two different tales: a morning of frustration and an afternoon of enjoyment. After nine hours on the river, the final tally was five fish caught for me and 11 for Todd. Not exactly a banner day, but you know what they say: a day of fishing is better than getting conked on the head with a frying pan.

When we left the restaurant later that night, after a meal graciously paid for by Todd as thanks for hosting the fishing weekend, it was raining hard. During the night we both were awakened with leg cramps, but fortunately for me we were in separate rooms, because Todd said his cramps were almost as bad as his Stinkytown, Wyoming hotel-room episode of last October. One of Todd's theories regarding the cramps is that constantly balancing on slippery rocks in the river puts a lot of stress on the legs. I imagine standing in cold water for hours doesn't help.

Leg Cramps and Snowy Roads

On Sunday morning the sky was heavily overcast and a check of the forecast showed that rain was inevitable with snow possible. But our route home had a 100% chance of snow starting at 10 a.m. and lasting all day. We agreed to postpone Sunday fishing, turning our fishing weekend into a fishing day. We left the house rather hastily at 9 a.m. to try to beat the weather home, with me accidently leaving last night's leftover dinner and a half-gallon of milk behind in the refrigerator. I can't wait to deal with that the next time we're there. I left the truck behind for the season and rode back with Todd. A stop at a popular coffee shop for "a quick cup" delayed us 20 minutes and by the time we had driven 25 miles we ran into snow.

At first it wasn't sticking to the road, but after another 20 miles it was, and the road became slick. I was worried that Todd's leg cramps would come roaring back to life, causing him to spastically jam down on the accelerator, sending us spinning into oncoming traffic, or plunge us into the icy creek that flowed alongside the slippery road. Todd apparently had the same concern because he slowed the car down considerably, which led to a line of traffic backing up behind us. On the bright side, if we did careen into the frigid waters there would be plenty of witnesses to tell the police what happened.

Good Grief!

The first Saturday of May promised to be sunny and pleasant, so Kathy and I drove up to Golden Gate Canyon State Park from our Denver home. Within 50 minutes of leaving the house, including a stop for gas, we were at the 7,800 ft. trailhead, me with my fly rod and Kathy with her camera. A short, undulating hike of less than 1.5 miles through the low mountains and tall pines brought us to a sloping meadow that held an old homesteader's cabin and a few outbuildings, with a small lake conveniently situated right in front of the place. As I assembled my rod and tied on a couple of flies, I kept an eye on Kathy, who was searching for a way to cross the creek that rushed into the lake so that she could get to the old, log buildings on the other side. Finally she found a narrow spot that she was able to jump across at about the same time I was ready to make a cast.

As soon as my flies were in the water I had a strike, but what looked to be an 11-inch rainbow trout quickly escaped. My second cast elicited a strike also, but this fish was quite small, perhaps eight inches. After being on the line for maybe 10 seconds it jumped out of the water and straight at me, landing in a small willow bush that separated me from the lake. *Well there's something new.* In the process the fish managed to dislodge the hook, but it was still wedged in the willow branches about 18 inches above the shore. When I reached for it, it managed to flop itself out of the bush and back into the water before swimming away. I gave it a 9 for difficulty, but only a 5 for technique.

I figured the fish were hungry since the ice had probably just recently melted off the lake. But after 15 minutes of no more strikes I decided that the remaining fish in this area were spooked from all of the sudden commotion. I reeled in my line and walked about 25 yards to where a log crossed the outlet of the lake. I wanted to get to a long stretch of shoreline that was unobstructed by backcast-snagging willow trees. The problem however, was that the log, perhaps stable under normal conditions, was now excessively wobbly from the rushing snow melt. Earlier I had watched as two fit and streamlined young women had tested the log and decided against crossing it. I don't know why I thought a middle-aged, decidedly un-streamlined guy such as me could cross the log. But I put one foot on the log and ... that's as far as I got. If there was a bear chasing me and my life depended on crossing it I certainly would have. Although I imagine crossing a six-foot wide, two-foot deep stream would have little benefit in a bear race. Fortunately a bear was not chasing me, so I saw no reason to risk slipping in and being uncomfortable in wet hiking boots and pants the rest of the day.

I looked around the rest of the lake and the only other spot that looked accessible and fishable now had a man and woman fishing there, he with a fly rod, she a spin caster. So I went back to where I had been fishing and tied on a different nymph, hopeful that something unlike the original nymph would prompt a strike. And it did, but this rainbow was also quite small. Kathy was back by now from her exploration of the log buildings and when she saw that I had a fish on the line she grabbed her camera. "Don't bother," I said. "It's really small." I did get this one in the net, but it was only seven or eight inches long.

We decided to eat the sandwiches we had brought along, so I followed Kathy to the cabin, crossing the inlet stream at the spot she found earlier. The cabin had a covered front porch that overlooked the lake, with two wooden porch-swings, one on each side of the doorway. We sat down on a swing and leisurely ate our lunch, enjoying the mountain views and watching the man and woman fish. After lunch I looked for a way to cross yet another inlet stream, still hopeful to reach the long stretch of lakeshore that promised snag-free fishing. The high, rushing water made a crossing impossible, so I decided to fish a narrow opening between willow trees that opened to a small slice of the lake.

I fished here without incident or fish for perhaps 10 minutes before my luck ran out. In trying to cover a little more of the lake, I attempted to expand the wedge of water I could reach and of course got my flies hung up in a willow tree on my forward cast. *Crap.* My hope for a quick retrieval and recovery was dashed when I realized that not only were both flies snagged, but my leader was wrapped around several small branches well above my reach. I leaned into the tree and bent the flexible branches down to where I could reach the leader and flies. But the branches suddenly slipped out of my grasp and sprang back to where they belonged. The fly line made an unearthly whipping noise and spiraled around me like a Slinky. When all motion stopped – tree, line, me - I inhaled deeply and took stock of the situation. *Crap!* I was indeed wrapped up inside my fly line like an overgrown enchilada. *Well, this is embarrassing.* But as I began to disentangle myself by trying to spin out of it counterclockwise, I saw that the line that held me captive was also hopelessly wrapped around the tree. *Seriously?!* I felt like Charlie Brown tangled up with his kite in the kite-eating tree. But I could see a way out of this. While I spun myself counterclockwise, the tree would have to spin clockwise.

Kathy, who had been watching my laughable antics from the porch swing, appeared and offered to help. I handed her my rod but in the process I felt a pinch in my right hand. I looked down to see that one of my flies had come loose from the tree and had hooked my index finger. Luckily it was the small nymph, and even though the hook had gone into my finger and curved back out again, the portion of skin it held hostage was shallow. Still entangled in fishing line and wrapped up in the tree, I grabbed my hemostats with my left hand and reversed the hook out of my finger. *Ouch!* I told Kathy she could set the rod down, no longer fearful that a pull on the rod would mean the amputation of my finger. When she did my leader snapped, which was a relief because by now I was looking for an excuse to quit fishing for the day. The broken leader also made it easier to extricate myself from the tree, unwind myself from the line and yank my flies from the tree.

I looked around to see if anyone had noticed me tying myself up in a tree. The couple fishing nearby may have been blocked by the willows, and another couple that had taken up residence on the cabin porch may have been blocked by a big pine tree. I thought back to see if I had cried out during the episode; something that would have given me away, like one of my patented yells of "crap!" or perhaps "Mommy!" But the telltale "try-not-to-make-eye-contact-with-the-doofus" look I got from the other couples told me that my swallowed-by-a-tree adventure was now indeed common knowledge among our fellow lakeside visitors.

The Kids are Alright

A mid-May Friday found us at little Haley's pre-school graduation ceremony, which was without a doubt the highlight of my day. Especially when compared to the fishing that came later. After the nineteen preschoolers regaled us with song (think "Wheels on the Bus"), artwork and a pot-luck lunch, we drove through Colorado's Front Range under a cloudy, gray sky. But it wasn't raining when we got to Chaffee County, so Kathy said she would get us unpacked and organized for the weekend if I wanted to go fish. *OK, if you insist!*

I was on the water by 5 p.m., fishing a large terrestrial as an indicator and trying various nymphs below. Even though I was trying to keep the rig simple, I was once again frustrated by tangles. And although the Prince of Darkness and Rainbow Warrior patterns I used provided a little success last time out, this time I was not so fortunate. By 7:30 the gray sky had turned dark enough that I was having a hard time seeing my fly on the water. I climbed out of the river, trudged up the bank and wound a quarter mile through the piñon-pine trees back to the truck.

Before driving off I paused to take a long pull on my water bottle just as a herd of 11 mule deer entered the clearing where I was parked. They paid me no mind as they leisurely crossed the path I had just walked, including two fawns that were playfully nipping at one another as they scampered through the piñons. My tangled-line, fishless-day frustrations melted away as I watched the deer and realized what a great day it had been. I had seen my granddaughter graduate from pre-school, I spent several hours fishing in a secluded, scenic spot, and now I was watching young deer frolic just a few yards in front of me. I'm not sure how life could get better. By actually catching some fish I guess.

Shimmy Shimmy Head-Conk Bop

Saturday morning was cool but sunny, with rain forecast for the afternoon. I took advantage of the weather by shimmying into the pitch-black crawl space beneath the house wearing a dust mask and hard hat on another carpet-beetle reconnaissance operation. This time I was armed with two brand-new, but cheap-ass halogen work lights I had purchased at a discount tool store. Unfortunately the electrical cords on the lights were only 12 inches long, not 12 feet as I thought I had read on the box. Another surprise upon opening the box was all the warnings about how hot these lights get. The caution labels that were stuck to almost every square inch of the lights basically said that if you use these you will almost certainly catch something on fire. By the time I rounded up and plugged extension cords into the stupidly short 12-inch-long cords, I still had one light uncomfortably close to the insulation along the house foundation. The insulation that hung down from the rafters in the shallow crawl space was also disturbingly close to the lights as they sat on the dirt floor.

I crawled on my hands and knees for about 20 feet from the small entry door to the area directly below the bug-room, conking my head on each beam I squirmed past, knocking the hard hat askew and prompting forth a string of expletives that, by the third time, I began to thread together so that they rhymed. It was inadvertent at first, but became sort of a head-throbbing, cloudy-vision, hip-hop lyric challenge the further I ventured into the subterranean, mouse-infested spider pit. By the time I had reached my destination, my lightheadedness had me convinced that I had a hit song on my hands.

The plan was to remove and discard the insulation along the two-foot-high foundation wall, hoping this was ground-zero for the carpet beetle larvae. With constant glances over my shoulder, expecting each time to see the insulation nearest the lights erupt into flame, I pulled out the insulation beneath the bug room and stuffed it into garbage bags. In my hunched-over, bent-neck position I couldn't really tell if the insulation was the carpet-beetle breeding ground or not.

What I could see were pockets filled with mouse turds near the top of each piece of insulation. I could also see by the harsh glare of the cheap lights, which had heated the crawl space to the same comfort level as a Phoenix parking lot in August, that the limited air of the crawl space was now choked with churning insulation fibers and mouse-turd dust. Hopeful that the inexpensive dust mask I wore would protect me from whatever nasty diseases were swirling around my face, I continued until I had two large garbage bags filled with varmint-infested insulation.

Desperate for cool, fresh air, I crawled back to the small opening, dragging the trash bags behind me and praying they wouldn't ignite as I passed the lights, which by now were roughly the same temperature as the surface of the sun. Thankful that I only smashed my head into a metal overhead beam twice on the way out, I emerged into the yard hacking up whatever evil crap I had swallowed like a cat with a bowling-ball sized hairball.

After alternately spitting out crawl-space gunk and sucking in the wonderful fresh air while watching Kathy do yard work for ten minutes, I reluctantly crawled back into Satan's sauna to finish the job. This time I carried with me some bug spray just to see how truly uninhabitable I could make it down there. After stuffing two more giant garbage bags full of the nasty-ass insulation, I sprayed every square inch of surface I could think of that may be inviting to our friends the carpet beetles. I retreated hastily through the resulting noxious cloud toward the crawl-space opening, once again dragging the garbage bags and this time turning off the lights as I passed them. After tossing the bags into the yard, then waiting for the poison cloud to dissipate and the molten lights to cool, I reluctantly climbed below ground once again, this time to retrieve the lights and conk my head once more for old time's sake.

The sunny morning gave way to clouds and by the time we had finished lunch we were surrounded by obvious storms. But after an hour, when we still had not been clobbered by weather, I headed out to fish the river. I started at the same spot I had fished yesterday, convinced I could do better. It turns out I was right, but just barely. Within 15 minutes I caught a 12-inch brown trout on a purple Psycho Nymph. The next hour brought two more fish to the line, but I unintentionally let them both off with just a warning, including one that entertained me with an aerial spectacle of acrobatics before freeing itself.

After a dry spell I began to switch out flies in an attempt to find something to entice a strike, but without success. The wind picked up and blew cold and hard enough that I put on a stocking cap and gloves, but I still didn't get the hint and continued to fish. When a driving snow unexpectedly hit I finally decided it would be a good time to stop for the day.

Strike Four

We pulled up to the mountain place at around 11:30 a.m. on the last Saturday in May to a beautiful, sunny and calm 61-degree day. After lunch I stopped by the fly shop and was disappointed that the usual young guy wasn't there, but instead an even younger kid. I told him where along the river I was planning to fish and he dispensed his advice with confidence. I thought *well, maybe he knows what he's talking about.*

I drove upstream to a favorite spot I hadn't fished in a while, but after parking the truck and walking 250 yards I realized I forgot my water bottle. *Crap.* I stopped walking and looked toward the river another half mile off and then I looked back toward the truck. *Do I really need the water bottle?* As I stood there trying to make up my mind, I looked down at my feet and saw a bear print, captured when the soil had been wet and now perfectly preserved in the dry ground. I reflexively looked over my shoulder and spied what used to be a young deer, its small, mangled carcass now consisting of mostly just the hide. Now whether that deer was killed by a bear, or maybe a mountain lion, made no difference. If I was going to be attacked by either one I'm sure I would be glad I had some water with me as I lay bleeding to death in the trees. I walked back to the truck for my water.

My first fly hit the river at 2:30, a big, double-bead Golden Stone with a Prince of Darkness two feet below that as recommended by the fly-shop kid. The first run was

136

unproductive so after a minor tree-snagging incident I moved up to a big, good-looking pool with a nice riffle running down the middle. I got a nice drift on my first cast here and my indicator stalled briefly. *Was that a strike?* I set the hook, but tentatively, and yes, fish on! But it didn't take long before the fish worked free, I assume because of the soft set. *O.K. let's try this again.* The indicator stalled very slightly on my next drift and this time I was deliberate with my hook-set. After a fight of several minutes I netted a wide, 15-inch brown trout.

I pulled three more fish out of this pool, fishing it for 45 minutes before finally moving upstream. Little did I know that these would be the only fish I would catch all day. I fished for two more hours without so much as a fishy nod in my direction. But it had been a gorgeous afternoon among awesome scenery, and despite an awkward, backhanded cast all day as I fished with my left arm toward the river, I had no major tangles and no snags other than the insignificant occurrence at the start. And hey, I wasn't slithering through a 400-degree crawl space breathing in insulation dust and worrying about black-widow spiders. And by the way, as a bonus, I caught four trout.

When I got back to the cabin, there was a deer in the yard. It completely ignored me as I pulled into the drive just a few feet from where it stood casually grazing. I sat in the truck and watched as it walked right by my open window, close enough to touch. It eventually moved on, so I took the opportunity to go into the house to grab a cold beer before coming right back outside to enjoy the mountain view from the deck.

Rocky Mountain Way

After the long winter and the cool and very rainy spring we almost forgot how beautiful the weather could be here. When the bright sun warmed the cool Sunday morning air we headed out for a slow, casual stroll along the river, watching the kayakers practice their maneuvers as we walked. At the furthest point of our walk, where we usually circle back toward the house, Kathy pointed out a boulder in the middle of the river that was hollowed out on top like a bowl. She had walked by here yesterday as a few young men were trying to throw rocks into the giant bowl, and they invited her to join them. We spent several minutes today, from our location up on the path, trying to throw rocks a fair distance across the river and down into the big rock bowl. (Isn't that the name of the bowling alley on "The Flintstones?" Big Rock Bowl?) A few of our rocks struck the boulder, but none of them actually went into the opening, most falling short or flying off to the side. It didn't take long to exhaust the supply of good throwing-rocks, presumably because most of them were flung into the river yesterday.

In the afternoon we headed to Castle Rock Ponds, a place that supposedly held cutthroat trout - according to the Colorado Parks and Wildlife website. After ten or fifteen minutes of highway driving we pulled off onto a dirt county road that curved through green meadows surrounded by rolling, pine-covered hills, many of which were topped with interesting rock outcroppings. Five or six miles later we found the ponds and pulled off the road, but the beautiful day was quickly giving way to threatening clouds.

We got out of the car nevertheless, me with my fly rod and Kathy with her camera. While she worked to photograph the pleasant scenery reflected in the four small ponds, I casted a large grasshopper pattern that was still on my line from yesterday, hoping to entice a strike from a big, old trout that was tired of the tiny bugs hatching everywhere. But the hopper looked like a battleship in a bathtub and besides, I saw no trout in the clear water longer than about three or four inches. What I did see was vegetation, rising above the waters surface along the edges and coming up almost all the way to the surface everywhere else in the pond. As I peered into the water trying to spot a decent-sized fish it began to rain.

We retreated to the truck and enjoyed what we could see of the view out of the rain-splattered windshield, including the snow-topped Buffalo Peaks. The rain lasted less than 10 minutes and when it stopped we hopped out to continue our activities. Kathy climbed a nearby hillside for a better vantage point to photograph Buffalo Peaks and I walked over to the next pond. This one was so jam-packed with vegetation I didn't even try a cast into it, certain that I would get snagged and probably break off my leader.

So I walked to the next pond, this time finding a spot where a stream flowed into it, thinking if there were fish here they would be lined up feeding on whatever was flowing into the pond. I did not see any fish rising to pick off any of the thousands of tiny bugs hovering over the surface, but I wasn't about to offer a nymph in the vegetation-choked subaquatica. I did remove the gigantic hopper from my line and tied on a small dry fly that I don't know the name of. A Fuzzclunker I think, or perhaps a Pubecruster. Whatever it was it was kind of a generic pattern that was just a little larger than the real bugs darting around. I still figured that my only chance was to offer something irresistible. It was not irresistible enough however, and after 10 minutes of plopping it out into the pond I reeled it in and walked back toward the truck, skirting the shoreline of two ponds and keeping an eye out for rising fish.

Back at the truck, as I waited for Kathy to climb down from her hillside perch, I scratched Castle Rock Ponds off my mental fishing list, although I wouldn't hesitate to return here for other stuff. What kind of stuff I don't know, just not fishing.

We stopped in town for a "healthy" frozen yogurt, piled high with enough fattening sweets to clog several arteries, before heading back to the house. Before long I decided to fish the river, returning to the scene of my Art Garfunkel tangle of 10 weeks earlier. I was struck by how quiet it was here and how private it felt, huge boulders separating this large pool from the strong flow just upstream. The river was considerably higher than my last time at this spot and not as clear. I hoped this would work to my advantage by the fish not being able to see me bumbling around above them.

I started a little below the big pool, casting a large Golden Stone and a green Prince Nymph into a flat spot below a small riffle. Bam! Fish on! It surprised me by swimming upstream, right into the next spot I was planning to fish before working the main pool. I followed it upstream, fearful that it would continue on to the large, quite pool and spook all those fish. So I was pretty aggressive in bringing it to the net, taking a chance that it would break off. Luckily it cooperated - the fine-looking 13-inch brown trout landing squarely in my net. Upon being released it wasted no time in swimming as far away from me as possible.

By now I was within easy casting distance of the main pool, but after several casts into what I thought was a likely lane I had no takers. *Hmm. OK, well try another lane then, Chris.* I casted a couple of feet to the left and watched as the mellow current brought the flies back toward me. I was almost hypnotized by the still air and gentle water when suddenly my indicator disappeared below the surface. I stirred from my stupor in time to set the hook and wham! My rod quivered and bent and before I knew it a large rainbow crashed through the surface of the tranquil water and flipped through the air. I gave this fish all the time it needed, which was a fair amount, and paid particular attention to keeping the line tight, before attempting to net it. Once in the net I measured it with my newish measuring-zinger dealy: a chubby 16 inches, a large fish for this water.

I caught another nice fish in this pool, a brown trout, before moving upstream, where I caught another brown. But when I caught no more fish after another hour I decided to step out of the river, thrilled to have had an all-around great day in the Rocky Mountains.

Gunk Scuz

We returned to the mountain place the following Saturday morning – the first weekend of June. The first order of business was to drain our water pipes. Before leaving last Monday we poured a strong bleach and water mixture down the well, and then turned on all the faucets in the house, including the dishwasher and washing machine, in order to sanitize our water supply and pipes. The last time we did this, which was also the first time, was last fall when we left the bleachy solution in the pipes for little more than 24 hours. Unfortunately the subsequent water-quality test had shown little improvement in the coliform bacteria level. So for the past nine months we have been brushing our teeth with bottled water, washing our fruit in Denver before bringing it with us, and worrying about what we were showering and washing our dishes in.

But this time, now that it was finally warm enough to leave the household water supply turned on without concern for bursting pipes, we left the bleach in the pipes for five days, determined to obliterate whatever gunk was scuzzing up our water. It took a surprisingly long time of running the water before it flowed without smelling like bleach. But it turned out our efforts had done the trick this time. The water-quality report from our sample, which arrived a few days later, showed a total coliform bacteria level of 0.

Laurie joined us for this weekend, and after lunch and a brief cloudburst, she and Kathy left for a walk along the river. I declined to join them, anticipating that I would fish. But with the river high, fast and muddy from snowmelt runoff I just couldn't get enthused about it. It sounded too much like work. Instead I decided to relax around the house, but before I knew it I was laboring in the warm sun.

First I pulled some weeds from around the deck and then I tackled a more ambitious project: building a step along the side of the deck with a giant piece of flagstone that was surplus to our Denver house. When I finished that I built two smaller steps at a couple of other deck-stepping-off points, then pulled the hammock out of the shed and set it up for the season in the shade of a few piñon trees. I carried the bench out of the shed, hosed it off and set it by the fire pit, and then turned my attention to the horseshoe pit, pulling a few weeds and raking the crusted–over-from-winter sand. There was still a couple of hours of daylight left and I once again considered fishing, but by then I was just too tired, electing to take a hammock nap instead.

Flying Wallendas

Kathy, Laurie and I had hiked to Brown's Creek Falls several years ago, which at that time either did not have a name, or we didn't know the name. As a matter of fact we didn't even know there was a waterfall at all when we started the hike, and probably still wouldn't know if we hadn't run into a helpful fellow-hiker. We wound up calling it Full Moon

Falls because two of us were mooned by the third. I won't mention any names other than to say Kathy and I were the moonees and not the mooners.

With unseasonably cool and comfortable June weather, we decided to hike to the falls once again, hopeful that the late season snow and recent rains would make it even more impressive than it had been during our previous trip in August. We pulled up to the trailhead at 10:30 Sunday after a half-hour drive from the house. Although still not mentioned at the main trailhead-signage, this time the occasional way-finding signs pointed the way and confirmed the existence: three miles to Brown's Creek Falls. The first mile and a half provides the occasional view out over the Arkansas River valley as it climbs from 8,870 ft. to 9,600 ft. over rocky terrain. I moved fairly slowly through this section, the rust of a long winter making itself known to my legs and lungs. The second half of the hike levels off and meanders through a pine forest that generally follows Brown's Creek, at one point emerging into a wildflower-filled meadow overlooked by snowy mountain peaks.

Once back in the trees the trail crossed the creek a couple of times before we heard the unmistakable roar of the falls. We continued up the trail as the sound of the rushing water grew louder. But after we passed a group of 8 or 10 young adults resting in a small clearing, the sound begin to grow fainter. Only when we back-tracked to the clearing did we see the sign that pointed the way off the main trail and to the falls. The sign was easy to miss. The faded word "falls" was carved into a weathered board that was only 12 inches above the ground and was mostly covered by a pile of rocks that were there to hold up the rickety signpost. In no way was I distracted, as has been suggested, by the ample cleavage of the female hikers we encountered here. That's my story and I'm sticking to it.

Another 50 yard climb brought us alongside the plummeting falls, which crashed out of the trees and plunged 35 feet down into a frothy pool, before tumbling another 60 feet into the waiting creek below. It was really quite impressive, hidden in the trees with little fanfare and no publicity. We had the place to ourselves when we first got there, but we knew that wouldn't last long so we rushed to take some unobstructed photos.

Sure enough, within a few minutes some other hikers showed up, including one idiot who was by himself (probably because he was an idiot) and who promptly climbed up the precipitous, wet rocks alongside of the falls, several times clinging precariously just inches from the roaring cascade. And since that was not foolhardy enough he decided to tiptoe across fallen, rotten tree branches slick with saturated moss that spanned the rushing water at the base of the falls. I really expected this clown to slip any second, crack his head open and be carried away by the forceful flow, not to be seen again until he washed up at a shipyard near New Orleans. On the plus side, it was kind of like having our own private Flying Wallendas show, so we sat down on a rock to eat our lunch, well out of the way of anyone who may want to photograph the falls, while watching this moron try to kill himself. (The Flying Wallendas are a family high-wire daredevil act that have been entertaining for several generations. I played bass in a bar band for a while with a drummer who claims to have played drums for their act – presumably a long snare-drum roll while they performed their death-defying feats, followed by a cymbal crash upon completion. I still don't know if I believe him. On the other hand why would anyone make up something like that? If you're going to make up something about drumming, make it something interesting like, "I was in a band that opened for the Rolling Stones in 1976 and we partied backstage with Mick and Keith." And if you are writing a book, why in the world would you use an arcane reference that needs over 100 words to explain? And if your last name is Wallenda, wouldn't it be awful tempting to name your daughters Linda, Belinda, Glenda and Melinda? Your son of course would be Wally.)

Finally the climbing clown wandered off, probably because it was tapioca time back at the insane asylum. No sooner was he gone than a group of five hikers wandered up, sat on a large, sloping rock outcropping right at the base of the falls and fired up a joint, again thwarting ours and other hikers' photo attempts. I was surprised that they left right after they finished it, expecting them to spend much of the afternoon mesmerized by the hypnotic waterfall. We decided we had waited long enough so we quickly moved out to the rock they had occupied, having had time to realize this was an excellent vantage point to photograph the falls. We spent about 10 minutes here before moving out of the way so as not to muck up other peoples' photos.

The blue skies quickly turned gray, and as we headed back down the trail the thunder began to rumble in the distance and light drizzle began to fall. Fortunately, serious weather didn't materialize and we stayed dry on the hike out. On the drive back to the house we stopped at a new gourmet ice cream place (call it gourmet and you can charge four times as much). It was tasty though, and we enjoyed it while relaxing in a courtyard shaded by an old cottonwood tree.

The relaxing continued back at the house when I opened-up the umbrella over the patio table. We sat enjoying cold ice-water while reviewing our waterfall photos. Eventually we refreshed our beverages with something a little more interesting and I put some buffalo burgers on the grill. And so ended a mountain weekend that I did not fish at all, and I was just fine with that. It just seemed like too much work.

No Excuses

It is becoming a tradition to spend Father's Day weekend at the mountain place with Megan and Bronson and the kids, with Bronson's parents Ben and Lisa driving from southern Colorado to join us. This weekend turned out to be mellow, relaxing and very enjoyable, despite the fact that I again did not fish. Well, not in the usual fashion anyway. With the river still raging from snowmelt, I elected to spend quality time with the family instead. We took it easy around the house, walked along the river, relaxed in the hammock and threw horseshoes – with Ben defeating me twice in a row.

But the highlight of the weekend was taking Haley fishing. She had been curious – no, make that anxious - to fish since February when she inspected my fly gear and excitedly listened as I told her about catching fish with a fly. I pulled a kids Barbie spin-casting rod from the back of the closest and we all made tracks for the Buena Vista town park on a picture-perfect Fathers Day. As it turned out, the usually serene town pond was muddy and out of its banks thanks to the swollen Cottonwood Creek that flows through it. But Haley was not to be deterred, so we rigged the rod with some fresh Power Bait and flung it into the pond for at least an hour without any interest from the resident population. But I have to give Haley credit, she hung in there for a long time for a five-year-old, and was still optimistic that we would catch something long after I had given up hope. I wish she had caught a fish and was left with an awesome memory of her first time fishing. But now I have an excuse to take her again.

Ooh...Ahh... Part 1

After getting only three hours of sleep for some reason, we left for the mountains at 8 a.m. Saturday morning, July 4, hoping that most holiday revelers would be traveling on Friday. We must have been right because traffic was very light for a holiday weekend. A warm and sunny morning greeted us, and after unpacking and an early lunch I headed for the fly shop just looking for advice. But of course I wound up spending $33 on flies.

I went back to the house to gear up, and then drove 10 minutes to a favorite spot along the river. A brisk five-minute walk through the piñon trees, where the yuccas and prickly-pears were blooming, found me riverside where the wild roses, penstemons, chiming bells and scarlet gilia were showing off their summer colors as well. No, I am not smart enough to know what these flowers were when I saw them. But I am smart enough to look them up in a book later. The river was fast and wide from snowmelt, but clear to about 1-1/2 feet, and it looked fishable along the edges. Actually accessing those fishable spots was another matter, with the high water lapping at the streamside vegetation and enveloping anything resembling a shore.

I was hoping to keep things simple and I was anxious to get on the water as quickly as possible after a layoff of more than a month. So I tied on a single dry fly – a smallish stimulator-terrestrial thing with legs, perhaps a #16. I found a clearing where I had enough room to make a few short casts before stepping into the water - just to be sure I wouldn't be stumbling my way through a fish lane. With no sign of action I waded in and cast out along the edge of a riffle that bubbled its way through a mellow pool in the otherwise roaring river. No response, try again. Still nothing. *Hmm – if I were a fish that's where I'd be.* One more time and bingo! A fish swirled up to the surface and gulped my fly. Somehow I managed to lift the rod tip with the right timing, speed, force and direction to set the hook. Upon realizing something wasn't right the fish took off downstream and got into the fast current, refusing to cooperate with my efforts to bring it in. I followed it downstream as far as I could in the swift water and the fish finally tired enough to allow me to net it - a 12-inch brown trout, my first since April on a dry fly.

A few casts later in this same pool and another fish rose to my fly but I missed it. I got another rise on the next cast, possibly the same fish, but this time I hooked it. Again the fish ran downstream, but it parked on the bottom in front of a large rock and refused to budge. *Great, now what do I do?* Having no idea, I moved downstream of the fish, upstream, and perpendicular to it, alternately reeling in and giving a little slack. Finally, upon getting some slack, the fish swam out of its hidey-hole after several minutes and went downstream, where I was able to bring it toward the shore and net the 14-inch brown.

All told I caught seven fish in the first hour, all on that same dry fly. This is unheard of for me: seven fish in an hour. When I first started fly fishing I would have been ecstatic if I caught seven fish in a month. I guess the fish were hungry now that the river was finally calming down and clearing up from the snowmelt. And apparently I got really good advice from the fly-shop guy, who was not the regular guy but another dude – perhaps a guide. Unfortunately dark clouds rolled in and I had a hard time seeing that fly, so I switched it out for a larger hopper pattern. This was only marginally easier to see in the gray light and elicited no reaction at all, so after about 10 minutes I switched it out for a foam Yellow Sally.

While not as hot as that first fly, the Yellow Sally proved to be popular also. I caught several more fish, including yet another that employed the hunker-down-in front-of-a-rock routine. I utilized the same method on this one, still not sure if it was the recommended procedure, and landed the fish, this one smaller at 12 inches. While removing the hook I set my net on a large, fallen log along the shore. The swiftly flowing river grabbed my net-tether-bungee thing, which was laid out across the water but attached to the shoulder strap of my chest pack, and pulled the net off the log and into the river. I wasn't concerned though, knowing the net was tethered to my pack. After I released the fish I turned back to retrieve my net, only to see it swiftly floating away down the river, taking the stupid bungee thing with it. *How the hell did that come unhooked!?*

While I watched it barrel away toward Pueblo Reservoir, 120 miles downstream, I thought about how I never liked that net very much, with its ridiculously huge basket that snagged every bit of vegetation within a mile of where I walked with it on my back, and was deep enough to land a manatee. But it did cost $40 (I told you I was a cheapskate), not to mention the cost of replacing the magnetic-tether gizmo.

Continuing to wade upstream from where I stood looked formidable due to the high water and fast current, plus I was anxious to move beyond the bad-mojo, runaway-net area as quickly as possible. So I climbed out of the river, side-stepped up the steeply sloped bank and walked upstream while looking down at the river for fishable water and a path back down through the vegetation to reach it. After a couple hundred feet of winding my way through the trees I saw a spot that I recalled enjoying previous success. As a matter of fact the mellow pool, fed by a couple of bisecting riffles, had been a real honey hole on more than one occasion. I spotted a steep but traversable path back down to the river, but after a few steps I saw a spin-fisher at the bottom end of the pool. So I continued upstream, still well above the river, and after just a few yards navigated around a boulder the size of a Hollywood mansion that blocked my path.

Once past the huge rock I looked back down to the river and saw another spin caster fishing the top of the hole. He looked up at me at about the same time, probably alerted by the sound of me crashing through the trees like a boob. We exchanged pleasantries, the typical having-any-luck stuff, when suddenly two large, red dogs came out of the trees and bolted up the hill straight for me, barking as they came, before skidding to a stop just inches from my jugular vein. They stood snarling and baring their teeth at me while I tried to remain calm, before the guy finally called them off. So much for pleasantries. *Have a nice freakin' day pal.*

I continued upstream as quickly as possible without actually running from the dogs, and eventually made my way down to the river at a decent-looking spot. I caught three more fish without the net, including the only rainbow of the day – a little six incher.

The sky had been rumbling with thunder most of the afternoon and when it finally started to rain I retreated out of the river and began walking back to the truck. I almost stepped on a snake as it slithered across the sandy soil before disappearing between two rocks. I couldn't identify the snake, not even by looking it up later, because there wasn't time to get a good look at it. But being a semi-expert on snakes I would guess that it was either a Dodge Viper or perhaps a Monty Python. Once at the truck I heard a wild turkey call from somewhere in the trees. Or it could have been a cold beer calling from the house.

So let's see: I lost my net, lost the net tether, was almost attacked by two vicious dogs and had a close encounter with a snake. But it was all worth it because in three hours I caught 13 fish. While certainly not a world record it was my personal best, and it left me feeling pretty good about my evolving fly-fishing skills.

After dinner at the house, we put a few beverages in a cooler, grabbed the camp chairs and drove up a county road that overlooks much of the river valley from the east. We pulled off the road, walked a couple-hundred feet through a field dotted with piñon trees and set up our chairs so that we looked west across the valley to massive Mt. Princeton. Once the sky grew dark, and the mosquitoes announced their presence, the Independence Day fireworks show began. We sat alone, just us, the mosquitoes and the occasional bat, and mostly in silence, other than the booming from across the valley. Occasionally one of us would say "that's a neat one," or we would ooh and ahh together. It was the perfect end to another awesome day.

If it Ain't Broke...

On Sunday morning Kathy and I went to the annual Mountain Mania car show in Buena Vista, hosted by the Arkansas Valley Car Club, where they close off several blocks of Main Street and display well over one hundred classic and muscle cars. We went early, anxious to avoid the typical scorched pavement of the midday July sun. Our strategy paid off and we were awarded with a pleasant morning of strolling among the awesome rides.

I wasn't sure I wanted to fish today, thinking it would only be a disappointment after yesterday's bounty, but of course I did fish. Luckily I had access to another net, stashed away in the closet like so many things we're "holding" for Todd. But still I had to make yet another trip to the fly shop, this time to replace the net-tether that had floated away with the net yesterday.

I fished the same section of river once again, reasoning that if it wasn't broke I wouldn't fix it. By the time I got started the sky had turned even more overcast than yesterday, which made spotting the floating dry fly difficult. I wound up catching five fish, missed several more strikes, and had another four on the line that I let get away. I also stumbled on a riverbed rock at one point and took a tumble in the river. But my biggest boneheaded move of the day was when I took my sunglasses off my face and simply let go of them, thinking they were on a leash around my neck. They weren't of course and the river claimed them, carrying them downstream to reunite with my net at the bottom of Pueblo Reservoir. This is the reason I buy $20 sunglasses and not $200 sunglasses.

So it turned out I was right, the fishing was disappointing compared to yesterday. But a year ago at this time a five-fish day would have thrilled me. Hell, a five-fish day two days ago would have thrilled me. And if someone had told me I would catch 18 fish over two days I would have questioned their sanity.

German Shepherds and Bachelorettes

Two weeks later – mid July - I was on the river by 5:00 Friday afternoon after driving up from Denver, unpacking and making a trip to the fly shop for another pair of $20 sunglasses. I immediately took the leash off my reading glasses and put it on the new sunglasses. The river was considerably lower than it was two weeks ago, so I kept an eye out for the net and sunglasses I lost the last time here. One thing I didn't see was my fly.

I was fishing in the long shadows of the trees on the west bank, preferring this to squinting into the late afternoon sun from the east shore. I started with a Yellow Sally, and on an early drift I picked up the fly to recast as it drifted toward me. Little did I know that there was a small fish on the line, which I unfortunately flung through the air and bashed into a large boulder behind me. The little guy just laid there on the surface of the big, slanting rock and I thought it was dead. I waded over to remove my fly, but as soon as I picked it up the fish started to squirm a little. I put it in the water, still with the hook in its mouth and the fish, although it had little x's for eyes, began to show a little more life. As soon as I began to remove the fly it suddenly started squirming like there was no tomorrow, which was a real possibility. It squirmed so hard that I had to put it in my net just to remove the hook. Even so, I revived the fish before releasing it just to be sure, and although it swam away briskly, I imagine this fish came away from its ordeal with one hell of a headache.

With no more action on the Yellow Sally I switched to a small terrestrial. But this was even more difficult to see so I changed to a big, foam hopper with a Golden Stone nymph tied below it. I caught three more fish for a total of four over 90 minutes, all brown trout. Two were about 12 inches long, including one that had a missing pectoral fin. The catch of the day was a meaty 14-incher that rose for the grasshopper pattern. Oh, and since my reading glasses were no longer tethered around my neck in favor of the new sunglasses, I managed to lose the reading glasses in the river.

My friend Tucker came up to Chaffee County for the weekend, showing up at our place with his German Shepherd Helen about the time it got dark Friday evening. The night was calm and mild, so we decided to build a fire in the fire pit. Bronson and I had built the fire pit several years ago but we never used it until tonight. On the rare evenings when we're not too tired from the day's adventures, it seems like it's too windy for a fire. But it turned out to be a perfect, starry night to sit and visit around a wood fire with a cool beverage.

Tucker slept outside on the deck to keep his dog company Friday night. He said he didn't get much sleep because he was watching meteors criss-cross the sky for much of the night. I was hoping to get him on the river Saturday, but I think he was worried about keeping an eye on Helen while river fishing. I suggested a quick trip to Wright's Lake and Tucker initially agreed, but then recalled that he and Helen ran into some "mean dogs" the last time they were there. "How about we 4-wheel to a high-mountain lake?" he asked. We decided on Pomeroy Lakes, which Todd, my brother Dave, his son A.J. and I tackled last July 4.

We loaded up our fishing gear and a cooler full of water, and then as a courtesy to me Tucker produced a greasy, dog-hair-covered bed sheet from his car and covered the back seat of my truck to accommodate Helen. All but the final few miles of the trip were a piece of cake as we traveled paved roads, well maintained dirt roads and a not-as-well-maintained dirt road before coming to the rocky-as-all-hell path for the final climb to the lake. Apparently this last stretch upset the big German Shepherd's delicate sensibilities and we stopped several times to let Helen out for a run and a drink from the creek that flows through this steep, narrow and green valley.

When we finally made it to the small parking area for the 12,000 ft. lake there were several modified Jeeps there and one guy with what looked to be a stock, full-size pick-up who was tent-camping with his young son just feet from his truck. I should have asked the guy how he squeezed his truck through some of the tight clearances between trees and boulders in order to get up here. We did talk for a few minutes, us fellow non-Jeep owners, mostly about the danger of lightning while camping above tree line. He was unaware that four people had been struck by lightning, killing one, less than 24 hours earlier while hiking nearby Mt. Yale.

I didn't want to scare the guy, but I also told him about the father and son who were found dead in their tent near the Maroon Bells, apparent victims of a lightning strike, also not too far away as the crow flies. I found out later that those two had actually succumbed to carbon monoxide poisoning from a heater they were using inside their tent. A slightly better way to go perhaps, but probably small consolation for their family.

Tucker was dinking around at the truck, so I headed for the lake, but before I went too far I came across the jeepers, who apparently belonged to a Jeep club, sitting in camp chairs admiring the stunning view of the lake surrounded by 13,000 ft., snow-capped ridges. They asked me about the types of fish in the lake and then looked at me glassy-eyed when I told them. Either none of them were fishers, or they were in awe of my studly ability to get my 18-year-old stock SUV, complete with running boards, up a trail that more than one guidebook rates as difficult. Probably none of them were fishers.

I headed for two small ponds that sat just upstream of the main lake, remembering that Todd and A.J. had seen some large fish in one of them as our day was ending last July 4th. Helen, who also got tired of waiting for Tucker at the truck, caught up to me as I reached the first pond. She playfully jumped into the water as I stood at the edge looking for fish. Not seeing any, I walked along the shore toward the second pond, continuing to look for fish as Helen splashed her way along the shoreline.

The second pond was larger and deeper and to my untrained eye looked more "fishy." The most direct route through the low, marshy vegetation brought me right up to a narrow, shallow stream that flowed into the pond. The path of least resistance to the pond was to step over the little stream and then follow it downstream 25 yards or so to the pond shore. I came to a stop to determine the best spot to cross and was surprised to see several fish facing upstream to feed, the crystal clear water just barely deep enough to keep them submerged. But just as soon as I spotted them Helen came bounding up behind me and crashed into the creek, sending those fish, and at least a dozen more that I hadn't previously spotted, scrambling for cover. By now Tucker was making his way toward the main lake and called out to Helen from a low ridge on the other side of the pond. Helen splashed around in the creek for several more seconds before running off to join Tucker, leaving a couple dozen scared-shitless fish in her wake.

Nevertheless, I couldn't resist the sight of all these fish - they looked like cutthroats to me – actively feeding in clear, shallow water right at my feet. I crossed the stream as quickly and stealthily as I could, which is to say me and my gear jumped across with all the grace of a cow being attacked by a rattlesnake. I walked downstream for several yards – toward the pond – before tying on a small terrestrial fly and tossing it upstream. Two things happened when I did: a truckload of fish in the pond behind me scattered as soon as I made my backcast, and my fly did not land in the narrow stream on my forward cast, instead getting snagged on the overhanging greenery. And despite creeping through the swampy muck on my hands and knees to un-snag my fly, as soon as I reached for it the fish once again scattered like dead leaves in a windstorm.

I went through this exact same routine several times before actually landing my fly in the stream and when I did, the fish bolted as if I had dropped a cinderblock into the quiet brook. I tried casting into the stream several more times, usually getting caught in the low, dense bushes along the edges. On the rare occasion when the fly actually hit the water, the fish by then just ignored it, although it practically bumped several of them in the nose. When the wind came up, turning my chances of a successful cast into the stream from highly-unlikely to no-freakin'-way, I turned my attention to the trout in the pond.

Despite casting from my knees in a ridiculous effort at subterfuge, the pond cutthroats that were lined up facing the inlet stream fled when my fly hit the water the first couple of times. After that, like their stream buddies, they just ignored me. So I switched flies and that was also disregarded. After a half hour of being ignored like the high school AV-club president at cheerleader practice, I finally realized: *I think they're on to me.* I casted further out into the pond a few times before it started to rain. As I was digging through my backpack for my rain jacket a strong gust of wind blew my hat into the pond. *This sucks!* But the hat floated long enough for me to retrieve it, and then 10 seconds after I put the jacket on and zipped it up, it stopped raining. *Hey, maybe my luck is changing!*

I decided to start fresh by walking briskly to the main lake, but I did cast into the pond a few times as I went. When I reached the outlet of the pond I saw a couple of dozen more cutthroats actively feeding in the shallows. This time *I* ignored *them. How do you like that, cheerleaders?* I followed the outlet stream 75 yards or so to the big lake, watching trout scatter with each step I took. As I approached the lake I bent low, staying back from the edge in an attempt to not give myself away. The water here was deeper and not as clear so I had renewed hope of catching a damn fish. After my first few casts the surface of the lake began erupting like Jiffy Pop popcorn on a hot stove. The fish had started jumping through the surface and splashing down like the ice we threw into our Cokes as kids. I felt like "Flounder" in the movie "Animal House:" *Oh Boy, is this great!*

But after two more casts it suddenly began to sleet - a thick, sideways-blowing sleet that stung my bare hands and face like gravel in a tornado. Not that I've ever been in a tornado, but you get the idea. It was all I could do not to yell out *ouch, ouch, ouch* with each impact. I reeled in my line and high-tailed it for the truck, a half mile away across the now-hostile alpine tundra. I zigzagged my way through the shrubs for 50 yards or so when I suddenly remembered my backpack lying back at the lakeshore. *Crap!* By the time I backtracked for the backpack, (note to self: idea for a catchy pop song – "Backtrack for my Backpack." Make sure it doesn't sound like Jethro Tull's "Bungle in the Jungle,") and finally made it to the truck, the sleet had turned to rain and I was soaking wet and mud-covered from sloshing through the muck. (Note to self: another catchy pop song – "Sloshin' thru the Muck to the Truck." Too bad my friend Chuck wasn't along for the sake of the song.)

At the parking area Tucker was huddled up against the truck with Helen, wearing a holey silver poncho-thing that he said was a space blanket. I asked him how long he had been waiting and he said 45 minutes - long before the sleet storm started! The pathetic sight of Tucker shivering beneath what looked to me like a sheet of aluminum foil peppered with buckshot holes made me sorry that I hadn't brought the spare set of keys for him, or at least hidden my keys somewhere for him to access. After hurriedly gearing-down we took off down the mountain, the truck smelling strongly of wet dog.

As we bounced over the rocks in the rain, Tucker said he had caught a fish, but was suspiciously vague on details about what kind of fish, how big it was or what fly he used. Tucker then said he was worried about Helen, who was looking nauseous in the back seat, so when the rain slowed they both got out to walk. Although he didn't admit it, I think Tucker was also queasy from the stomach-churning ride. They walked at about the same speed as I drove, crawling the truck down the rocky mountainside. When the rain increased they both hopped back inside, although we did stop a few more times to let Helen's (and probably Tucker's) stomach settle.

The weather cleared by dinner time so Kathy, Tucker and I went to a new restaurant in town, dining on the patio. It got a little cool once the sun dipped behind the towering peaks to the west, but we recovered nicely thanks to the distillery one block down. We had walked across the street from the restaurant to the "gourmet" ice cream place but en route we heard some interesting live music. It sounded like a classic Allman Brothers song but played in a rowdy, bluegrass style. We decided to ditch the ice cream and followed the sound of the music down the block.

We found a very lively patio scene at the local distillery, highlighted by what looked to be a bachelorette party dancing non-stop to an Americana-type band – upright bass, acoustic guitar, violin and drums - playing unique arrangements of classic rock songs without pause. Just as I was marveling at the stamina of the young, dancing women I noticed an old guy (and he had to be old if *I* call him old) keeping up with the women step-for-step. This guy had to be 80 years old, and I thought it was great that he was obviously having such a good time, but at the same time worried that he was going to keel over from a heart attack at any moment. When the female violin player broke into a solo, this guy danced exuberantly just inches from her, with nothing separating the two but her violin. We could hear her solo just fine, but all we could see was the back of this guy's bald head and quaking body. We stayed here for about an hour, nursing a libation, people-watching and enjoying the music, and the band never even paused, charging seamlessly from one song to the next, the bachelorettes and the old guy dancing wildly every second.

You're Fishing Wrong

After another night of sleeping on the deck with Helen, Tucker headed off for parts unknown on Sunday morning. And after a quick breakfast I headed for the river to try some streamer fishing. Todd had read something from a Denver-area fly shop earlier in the week that got him excited about fishing streamers. He had called me and said he was thinking about going to the shop to pick-up the recommended tackle and wanted to know if he should pick up this stuff for me too. I told him possibly, but I was on a bit of a fishing budget after having recently lost my net, sunglasses and reading glasses, so please call me and let me know how much this stuff would cost. He did call me back a couple of hours later and told me I owed him $30. *Huh? So much for calling with the cost first.*

According to Todd the guy at the fly shop had a can't-miss method for catching huge trout, which included a specialty leader, tippet and of course several exotic-looking and costly streamers. I caught a fish on a streamer once, a year or so ago, otherwise I've never had any success. Admittedly I didn't really know what I was doing, but still I found streamer fishing to be kind of monotonous. So on Friday morning I drove to Todd's office to give him $30 that I really didn't want to part with for some stuff that I didn't really want. When I got there Todd had the leader and streamers laid out on his desk along with a sketch from the fly-shop guy showing exactly how this rig was to be fished. *OK, this could be good, maybe I can finally learn how to fish streamers.*

Todd texted me a couple of times over the course of the weekend, anxious to know if I was having any luck with the streamers. So on Sunday morning I switched my leader for the new, sinking leader, tied on heavy tippet and two streamers as instructed – a large, sparkly yellow one and a larger, articulated black one - and walked from the house to the river. As I approached the water I saw a bike leaning against a tree, but I didn't see anyone fishing nearby so I cautiously stepped down the escarpment to the water. I followed the shoreline upstream until I ran out of public access, and clumsily casted the awkward rig into the river. Immediately, almost before the streamers hit the water, certainly before they had a chance to sink on the sinking line, a trout leapt through the surface, attacking the large, yellow streamer as if it were a dry fly. *Well, I wasn't expecting that.* Dumbfounded, I did not react in time to set the hook, which was unfortunate because that was as close as I would get to catching a fish all day.

But I dutifully fished this rig for most of the morning, casting downstream and across, letting the current carry the flies downstream a bit before swinging them back toward the close shore and then stripping-in line to simulate a small fish swimming upstream. I worked my way downstream in this fashion for two hours, meticulously covering every inch of water that I could safely reach. And guess what? It was monotonous. And boring. But I wanted to be able to report to Todd that I gave his "can't-miss" method a solid chance of success, and that it still sucked.

The highlight of the morning was when I came across the apparent owner of the tree-leaning bicycle, a glassy-eyed guy panning for gold. It was 10:30 in the morning and he was drinking a PBR tallboy, and he felt it his duty to tell me I was fishing wrong.

"You're fishing wrong. You wanna be casting upstream."

"Well yes, normally, but I'm trying these streamers and it has been recommended to me to cast them downstream, swing them across and then strip them back upstream toward me," I explained patiently.

He looked at me with his red eyes for a moment before saying, "Still, you wanna be casting *up*stream."

"Thanks for the advice." *And have another beer.*

Ooh...Ahh... Part 2

The plan for the first weekend in August was for Megan, Bronson and the kids, and possibly Bronson's parents, to join me and Kathy for the weekend. But little Kaden got sick a couple of days prior, understandably causing his parents to stay home with him. But Kaden's big-sister, five-year-old Haley, still wanted to come up to the mountains because she had been looking forward to Gold Rush Days in Buena Vista. This is the town's annual heritage celebration that features a burro race, 5k fun-run, simulated, old-time shootout and a two-day fair in the town park with live music, vendor booths, beer garden and stuff for the kiddies like a little train ride and "gold" panning.

Kathy took Haley to the fair early Saturday afternoon and I headed for the river. After parking the truck I walked down a path toward the river, quickly coming to a campsite right on the trail. Not off to one side, but right in the middle of the trail. Following the path brought me right through this campsite, which was littered with empty and full beer cans and featured a very dirty, wadded-up sleeping bag upon which strangely sat a can of gasoline, both of which I had to step over as I made my way to the river. Luckily I didn't see anyone actually camping there, and I wasn't about to announce my presence, fearful that some yahoo would start shooting from inside his tent for the indiscretion of walking through his delightful camp.

Once down at the river, an early cast hooked a very small brown trout on a huge grasshopper pattern that I was using more as an indicator to a much smaller dry fly tied behind it. And just like two weeks ago, my hook-set resulted in the small fry catapulting through the air and landing with a splash 25 yards downstream. At least it landed in the river this time, not slammed into a mid-stream boulder like before.

That was all the action I had for an hour, despite switching flies several times. I finally got a solid strike just as a couple of float-trip rafts drifted by. This was a substantial fish that had swallowed my fly while I had the rod pointing downstream and parallel to the water in an effort to extend the drift. The boaters oohed and aahed as I fought the fish, but with my rod flat to the water I couldn't lift the tip up high enough before the big fish broke free.

After an hour and a half of no further activity, despite switching flies frequently, a shiny, red nymph finally produced a strike, but once again it was just a little dude. Frustrated, I climbed out of the river after three-plus hours, having caught only two fish, each just six inches long. The walk back to the truck took me right back through the weird campsite, and once again I treaded quickly and quietly for fear of waking a shotgun-wielding maniac.

If Robert Plant Sang for Faces, Would the Band be Called "Face Plant?"

Because of the unusually snowy spring and rainy summer, the front "yard" of the mountain house was more overgrown than normal. I had been using a weed whacker to keep the "lawn" under control but that just wasn't cutting it any longer. Pun intended. The quotation marks around the words yard and lawn are to indicate that it's not a lush, green lawn in the suburban sense, but more of a rocky, sandy-soil, weed-choked lot with a couple of scrawny trees. So I finally broke down and bought a lawnmower for the place, and after picking up loose rocks with help from Kathy and Haley, I mowed the weeds down Sunday morning.

Kathy took Haley down to the river park to play in the water in the afternoon and then into town for frozen yogurt. While in town they watched some of the burro race – which is part of the Gold Rush Days festivities. A confused Haley later told me she thought it was going to be a "barrel" race. Apparently she expected people to climb into barrels and careen down a tree-studded hillside.

I fished the river of course, choosing a spot further north this time, just to mix things up and perhaps change my luck.

159

Once again a very early cast resulted in a rise to my giant hopper by a very small trout. I was able to hook, net and release it with no problems, but that would turn out to be a rare occurrence this day. The fish were rising to my flies with regularity, but I wasn't able to hook them. There were probably 20 fish that came up to have a look and perhaps that was the problem - they were just looking. I did manage to hook a few that flung themselves free with little difficulty, but mostly I came up empty when setting the hook.

Sometimes when I'm concentrating on the drift of my fly I'll forget that I'm standing in a river. A river with big, slippery rocks and unexpected holes and drop-offs. While I'm watching my fly or looking for the next spot to cast, or perhaps while I'm casting, I'll begin to move upstream. And when I forget that I'm in the middle of a river, like this time, the results can be embarrassing. I simply began to take a step upstream and immediately tripped over a shin-high rock, sending me face-first into the cold current.

After a couple of frustrating hours and three tiny trout, I finally came to a large pool that to me looked like it should be teeming with fish. *OK, I'll fish this pool methodically and if I don't net a fish I'm done.* I was a little tired by then, mostly from awkwardly casting backhanded in an attempt to avoid the cottonwoods and willows that lined the banks, so I added: *and if I do net a fish I'm done.* I switched out my huge hopper top-fly and smaller caddis trailing-fly for a fair-sized, elk-hair attractor. After a few casts into the bottom of the pool, I was able to climb into the river, unlike downstream where the water was deep enough that I had to fish from the bank. Finally with a right, over-hand cast, I felt more confident and was able to put the fly more-or-less where I wanted.

I dropped the single fly along the edge, working my way out toward the center with subsequent casts before stepping upstream and repeating the process. After 20 casts or so I got a solid strike and set the hook. The fish jerked in protest and took off running downstream for a cascade that defined the bottom of the pool. I was afraid it would swim down the cascade and lodge into the rocks at the bottom, so I worked to make sure the fish didn't get there. But this felt like a big fish so I decided I should let it run just a bit out of fear that it would easily break free otherwise. But when I gave it a little slack it quickly slid down the cascade and was abruptly off the hook. *Damn!*

I was only a third of the way up the pool so I continued systematically working it, relieved that large fish were interested in my fly selection. After perhaps another 20 casts, just when I figured that I had spooked all the rest of the fish in this pool, another fish unexpectedly surfaced. I set the hook, and even though the fly didn't hurtle back toward me, I didn't feel the usual opposing tug either. *What the hell?* I stripped in some line and suddenly there it was, a hard yank that bent my rod downward. I was further upstream from the troublesome cascade, so I was able to let the fish run and tire a little before attempting to net it. When I put the net in the water the fish freaked and made a last second run, but it couldn't go far with the short line it had. A second attempt at netting it was successful, my perseverance finally rewarded with a fit, 14-inch rainbow trout.

Tired, hungry and thirsty, after releasing this beauty I stepped out of the river and climbed up the bank, zig-zagged through the piñons and sage for 15 minutes to the truck and made a 10 minute drive to the house where a cold beverage had been calling me for at least an hour.

Strange Days Have Found Us

To say this mid-August weekend was bizarre would not do it justice. I'm not sure it can even be defined as a weekend. Let's just call it one really nice day followed by an inconceivably strange day.

Saturday promised to be a warm day when we pulled up to the mountain house at 11 a.m., so I cranked up the swamp cooler. After lunch I noticed that the water was draining from the cooler much faster than normal. Instead of the usual slow drip it was a constant stream. So I farted around with the damn thing for over two hours - removing the cover, adjusting the float, replacing the cover – over and over – without making a difference in the volume of the water overflow. *Screw it, it's cooling the house so I'll deal with it later – the fish are waiting.*

I geared up and drove upstream a little further north than usual, watching as a dark cloud moved in from the west. Just as soon as I parked the truck it began to rain hard, Mother Nature not bothering to mess with a sprinkle first and then a light shower. Just a sudden, driving rain that kept me hostage in the truck. In case you're wondering, this was the good day of the weekend.

Half an hour later the rain stopped as suddenly as it started so I hopped out and geared up at the tailgate. I had decided to fish behind a house that we tried to purchase several years ago, a deal that fell through before we bought our current piece-of-crap house. (That is a hint about the yet-to-come weird part of the weekend.) To my knowledge this house and other nearby homes do not own the property to the middle of the river, but instead there is a thin strip of public land along the river's edge. So I walked downstream perhaps a quarter mile, keeping a keen eye out for "No Trespassing" signs, until I was directly behind the house. The water looked good – a lot of structure and seams – but further downstream looked even better.

So I kept walking south, past one awesome-looking pool after another, watching closely for any indication that I was no longer on public land. Before long my route was blocked by a large fallen tree and the path of least resistance was to angle up the bank. And then I ran into thick foliage and had to slant up the bank even further. The next thing I knew I was walking on flat ground above the river channel, weaving my way through the pines, watching even more closely for any hint that I was trespassing. I saw no fences or signs or people or houses, just thicker vegetation and more pristine-looking land.

Eventually I came across an old stone-walled cabin with a caved-in roof. What I didn't see was a way through the heavy greenery back down to the river. By now I had been walking for 30 minutes and I was burning daylight, so I doubled my efforts to find an approach to the water. I finally came to a spot that was a little less steep and packed with fewer wader-snagging thorn bushes, so I plunged into the underbrush, landing at the riverside relatively intact and no worse for the wear.

From where I stood on the shoreline I saw a trickle of water seeping out of the riverbank that flowed down through lush, green moss and hundreds of shooting star wildflowers. Gigantic boulders formed deep pools along the shoreline and tiny fairies silently flew among unicorns and rainbows. OK, maybe not the last part. The point is that this was an unusually verdant spot, made neater by the fact that I had never been here. Indeed, it looked like no one had ever been here, except for whoever nailed the "No Trespassing" sign to the nearby tree. *Oh crap!* Well, the sign was downstream of me and I would be working my way back upstream, so there should be no problem. Unless of course I came across additional signs on my way upstream.

I tied on a foam hopper pattern and a small stonefly nymph a couple of feet below that, and casted into the large pool right in front of me. It generally takes me a few casts and drifts for my eyes to adjust to whatever the light conditions are so that I can consistently see and follow the fly once it hits the water. On my second cast, as I was searching for my fly, a trout gave me a pretty good clue when it crashed through the surface for the foam grasshopper. I flicked the rod tip up but came up empty. *Damn!* The next pool upstream however produced two brownies that eagerly ate the hopper.

I removed the nymph from my line at this point, having fun catching fish on the dry fly and thinking that I could get a softer landing and a better drift of the hopper without the nymph. I worked my way upstream through what appeared to be rarely fished water for a few hours, catching eight trout ranging from 11 to 14 inches, on assorted terrestrial patterns. I had a few more fish on the line that got off, and several other rises that I did not hook. I was a little nervous about the ownership status of the land I was fishing, but despite looking frequently for signs of private ownership I never found any. At one point my phone fell out of my chest pocket, which I had failed to zip, and plopped into the river. Luckily I was able to scoop it up quickly, and coupled with the modest protection of the sandwich bag I keep it in, save it from apparent damage.

By the time I was back upstream and behind the house we had tried to purchase, it was getting dark. I tied on my best-floating, most visible hopper pattern and it was rudely ignored close to the bank, where the fish had been active all day. But as I worked out further toward the middle of the river, suddenly the fish took notice. Despite a few rises I did not hook any more fish, the fading light and my weary mind and body working against me. When I could no longer see the fly I reeled it in and hustled to the truck, anxious to make it back before darkness fell and the bears and mountain lions started to roam. Despite wasting two hours not fixing the swamp cooler, and a half-hour watching from the truck as the rain fell, I had a great day fishing new water.

Since I had mowed the weeds around the house two weeks ago the "yard" actually didn't look half-bad. But there were still tall weeds around the trees and the shed that I couldn't get with the lawnmower, so I broke out the weed-whacker mid-morning Sunday. That chore completed within a half-hour, we went to the hardware store, me for a new swamp-cooler float valve and Kathy for supplies to paint the back door, which had strangely developed a funky, reddish-black stain right at eye level. Hopefully that's not an indication of a supernatural habitation or other ghostly apparition.

I changed out the float valve, which made only a marginal difference in the amount of water gushing out of the thing. And then, finally, I tackled the project that I had been putting off all weekend (here comes the bizarre part). Our five-year effort to eradicate the carpet beetles in the bug room – formerly known as the purple bedroom – has been a total failure. Despite constant carpet cleaning, bug-bombing the room and crawl space below, liberal applications of boric acid and even removing the carpet - all laced with copious amounts of profuse swearing - nothing has worked. Every summer from mid-June through mid-September the room is unusable because of a swarming invasion of the little suckers. Finally we decided we should cut out some drywall at what appeared to be ground zero to see if we found anything unusual, like a dead mouse, which the insects may be feeding on. Although based on the number of bugs and the fact that they have been here for at least five years, I suspected that a single dead mouse would have been consumed long ago.

We had removed a wainscot panel earlier in the summer in hopes that that they were somehow attracted to something between it and the drywall but we came up empty. So after I located the studs I painstakingly measured and cut out a 16-inch-square drywall section behind the missing wainscot, allowing for a quick and easy replacement of the removed drywall. It turns out there was no need for such precision.

When I pulled out the cut-drywall square I was greeted with an overpowering stench that almost made me throw-up in my dust-mask. And I was shocked to see, in there amongst the insulation - dog food! I cut the insulation at the top of the opening and pulled it out of the cavity, bringing with it at least two pounds of dry dog food. Whatever I yelled in alarm, which definitely was not "goodness gracious," brought Kathy running.

"Put your mask on," I urged when I heard her coming.

She took a look at the weird scene and asked "What is it?"

"Dog food."

"Dog food? How in the world did it get in the wall?"

"Mice, I guess."

"How did mice get in the wall?"

"From the looks of it I would say they drove in with a front-end loader filled with dog food."

"Where did the dog food come from?" she asked.

"I guess the previous owners had a dog."

"It must have been a wimpy dog if it couldn't keep a mouse away from its food dish."

Kathy brought me a trash bag and when she couldn't find a small gardening shovel she produced an old serving spoon. I scooped out the insulation/dog-food casserole from the wall cavity and upon reaching the bottom, found that the overpowering odor was from the mouse urine that soaked the mouse-crap-covered bottom plate. *Lovely.* After cleaning up that mess I cut out another drywall square right next to the first one. This time when I pulled the drywall away, a torrent of dog food ripped through the insulation and came pouring out onto the floor. There was at least twice as much as the first opening, and it spilled onto the floor like some kind of bad-dream waterfall. Every once in a while, when I can't believe it actually happened – which is about three times a day - I look at the photos on my phone for proof. And when I do the reeking vapor once again invades my brain through my now-ruined nasal cavity.

By the time I was done cleaning up disgusting mess number two I was livid. We had been tearing our hair out and working our asses off for five years because some incredibly lazy-assed slob didn't realize that their 10-pound dog couldn't possibly eat 50 pounds of dog food every week. If I found dog food behind the only two pieces of drywall I removed, what is hidden behind the walls in the rest of the house?

Later that night we watched a red fox bounding around at the far end of the property, presumably chasing a mouse. I felt a real affection for this fox, and any creature that would kill a mouse, after what mice had done to my house.

The next morning, Monday, we were enjoying our coffee as we stood looking out at 14,196 ft. Mt Princeton. A doe sauntered by the window with two spotted fawns obediently following, playfully nipping at each other as they bounced by. For a moment this peaceful little scene let me forgot about the freaking mice that had put the freaking dog food in the walls of my freaking house, and the freaking a-hole that allowed this to happen. But just for a moment.

Come On Baby Light My Fire

For the first time in five years I was not looking forward to our trip to the mountains this weekend, the last in August. I knew that the main objective would be to rip out the drywall along the entire south wall of the bug-room, remove the insulation and clean up the rotting dog food, the mouse crap and the revolting-smelling mouse urine that saturated it all. During the week I read up on Hantavirus, the wicked virus that can infect humans like me through contact with mouse droppings, urine or saliva, and can lead to nasty diseases that cause bad things like death. *Great.* So I bought the recommended N100 respirator and N95 dust masks, made sure we had bleach and rubber gloves, and checked that my life insurance was paid up.

No sense in putting it off, so upon arrival on Saturday morning I immediately put on the respirator and rubber gloves and began tearing out drywall. And as expected, with each piece I pulled away from the wall, a buttload of dry dog food came rushing out onto the floor. I sprayed everything I saw - insulation, dog food, drywall, mouse crap, wall studs – with a substantial coating of bleach solution as recommended by the "experts" and let it sit for an hour while we ate lunch.

After lunch I went back into the room armed with a full-size shovel and scooped up at least 30 pounds of dog food into trash bags. I chucked the insulation out the window where it piled up among the previously chucked drywall. The whole time I continued spraying bleach on anything that looked like a mouse could have come near it. I wound up removing the drywall, insulation and dog food 32 inches up from the floor along the entire south wall of the room – 16 linear feet. After bleaching-down everything once again I fastidiously swept everywhere, and once confident I had removed every ounce of suspicious material, I vacuumed the carpetless floor and inside the now-bare walls.

When I was done in the room I went outside and bagged up the disgusting mess, which was when Kathy pointed out that many of the discarded drywall pieces were covered on the inside surface with carpet-beetle larvae. I raked the ground for remnants and then hauled eight full trash bags to the shed to await transport to the dump on Monday morning, while Kathy sprayed the ground with bug-killer. I then set fire to the yard, the shed and the house and watched it all burn to the ground while laughing maniacally. Not really of course, but I was sure tempted. What I really did was saturate everything with bleach that I had used in that room – tools, shovel, broom, vacuum cleaner - threw my clothes in the wash, threw my shoes in the trash and threw myself in the shower.

Let Me be Clear

My plan for Sunday was to spend as much time as possible outdoors in the fresh air, as far away from the bizarre, dog-food-in-the-wall situation as possible. After breakfast we took our usual two-mile walk along the river under calm, cool and cloudless skies, noticing that some of the native bushes were already starting to wear their yellow and red autumn colors. Since I had banished the mouse-crap broom to the shed I made a trip to the store for a new one, and upon returning spent a fair amount of time talking over the fence with the neighbor. I finally left the house for the river around noon, by which time it had warmed up substantially. By 1 p.m. I was frustrated.

The river was as clear as I've seen it – deceptively clear. It made the water appear shallower than it was, which made for some surprising wading moments when I wandered into water that was deeper than it looked. Somehow I managed to keep my footing but since I elected not to wear my waders this warm afternoon, I was unpleasantly surprised by a couple of inadvertent dunkings of the ol' nether-regions.

But my frustrations stemmed more from the fact that I wasn't getting any reaction to my flies. I was hoping that this would be a banner day for dry-fly fishing – hell, the grasshoppers were everywhere. But after an hour of fishing various hopper and terrestrial patterns with only two tepid rises, I reluctantly tied on a Prince-Of-Darkness nymph below the dry fly. I say "reluctantly" for two reasons. I have come to enjoy the excitement of a fish suddenly splashing up to the surface to attack my fly, and the challenge of hooking it before it spits out the fly and quickly disappears. Much less exciting to me is watching to see if that top fly or perhaps a generic indicator dips or stalls in the water as an unseen fish swallows a tiny nymph well below the surface. The second reason I was hesitant to tie on a subsurface fly was because I'm just asking for tangle-trouble if I have more than one fly on my line.

After a few casts and drifts with the "hopper-dropper" set-up I picked up the line when the fly had drifted back to me and was surprised when a fish came with it, the Prince Nymph hooked into its upper lip. It was a small brown trout, no more than seven inches, and it just swung at the end of my line right alongside me, about waist high. I reached down into the river to get my hand wet before grabbing the swinging fish out of midair and then quickly unhooked and released it.

Little did I know that this would be the highlight of my fishing day.

I kept fishing this same set-up for a while, hopeful that I had hit on the right fly. But with no further strikes after 20 minutes I switched things up again. Eventually I found myself switching flies every 10 minutes or so purely out of frustration. I couldn't believe I wasn't catching fish on this beautiful day. After a while I noticed that my casting technique had become sloppy, so I concentrated on my casting, not wanting to lapse into bad habits.

The low water level meant that the commercial rafting outfits were done for the season and other recreationalists were taking advantage of the mellow flow and lack of big boats. Two stand-up paddle boarders drifted by at one point, the lead guy saying hello while confidently surfing by. The second guy was concentrating so hard on staying upright in the mellow flow that he didn't dare look beyond the front of his board.

Later on, while I was standing in the middle of the river at a spot where it is wide and shallow, a group of six inflatable kayakers came paddling downstream. They were real people, it was the kayaks that were inflatable. But they stopped just upstream when they saw me, apparently perplexed by my position in the river. They attempted to huddle together for a conference, while looking at me and looking at the mild water around me, presumably to determine how to deal with this unexpected obstacle. Their obvious inexperience was a hindrance to their mid-stream consultation however as they bounced into each other and got knotted up in a six-boat tangle. I felt like I was watching the Three Stooges, Lucy and Ethel, and Inspector Clouseau guest-starring on an episode of "Gilligan's Island." I said, "Um, I can move if I'm in your way."

They tried to act casual and one said, "No, it's cool," and then they all bumped and bumbled past me on their way downstream.

As I continued wading upstream, hopefully to a magical pool where the fish would eat everything that floated by, I came across a guy who was mineral prospecting his way downstream.

"How's it going?" I asked with a cheerfulness that belied my frustration.

"Mumble, mumble, mumble," was how I heard his response.

"Great! Well, take it easy."

"Mumble, mumble, mumble," he mumbled as he continued downriver.

After four hours of continuous wading and casting, only to come up empty, I reeled in my line and scrambled out of the river and up the bank. At the top of the bank I walked in a downstream direction, figuring I had fished my way well upstream of where I parked. I hiked through piñon trees and yellow-flowered rabbitbrush, my water-filled boots squishing with each step through the sandy soil. After a quarter mile or so I came to an area I recognized as being well downstream of where I parked. *Dang-it*, I had been walking the wrong direction!

So I walked even further out of my way to the access road so that I could follow it to the pull-out where I parked rather than continue my aimless wandering through the trees. By now my right boot had come untied and there was a hunk of gravel in there the size of a minivan. And for some reason, here in this boulder-strewn valley, there were suddenly no rocks to sit on while I took off my boot in order to remove the offending rock. So I just limped my way along the trail, my ridiculously long bootlaces flapping around and picking up every plant bur within a four-foot radius while my watery boots sloshed prodigiously, like I was walking on a waterbed. It wasn't until I finally found the truck that I realized what a great day it had been. Sure I only caught one little fish, pretty much by accident, but I had spent most of a beautiful, late-summer day outside along a scenic river. In my book that is a hell of a lot better than tearing out the walls of my house and shoveling urine-soaked dog food out of mouse-crap infested insulation.

Take Your Toddler Fishing

We elected to stay home over the Labor Day weekend and not fight the traffic to and from the mountains. Besides, we had just been up to Chaffee County the previous weekend and we needed more time away from the nasty, dog-food-in-the-wall situation. After breakfast on Sunday morning we decided to take a hike in Golden Gate Canyon State Park, located in the foothills west of Golden.

We reached the park within 45 minutes - after a stop for gas and winding our way up the two-lane, foothill road for 12 miles. Fifteen more minutes of driving to the far side of the park found us at the trailhead for the "Snowshoe Hare" trail. This looked to be a three-mile loop trail that just happened to pass a body of water called Dude's Fishing Hole. So I put my fly rod and chest pack into my backpack along with my camera, our lunch, rain jackets, extra water and since I may be fishing, Kathy's early generation (heavy) e-reader.

From the trailhead at 8,800 ft. elevation, the route took us mostly downhill through the trees, along a very rocky trail that appeared to be a series of dry creek beds. On the rare occasions that we climbed uphill, we found ourselves walking on loose rocks. Kathy and I have hiked in this park several times in the past, most recently in early May when we hiked to another small pond and I managed to entangle myself in a willow tree thanks to an errant cast. As a matter of fact, our first-ever hike together was at this park on a photography-class excursion.

But this Snowshoe Hare trail was much rockier than any of the others we had hiked here and the further we went downhill the more concerned we became about poor footing on a steep, uphill, return hike. A couple of times, as I cursed all the extra weight in my pack, I wondered if we were even on a trail, but each time a nearby marker would confirm that we were. The thought of getting in a little quiet fishing in a mellow mountain pond made the struggle more endurable.

After about 1.75 miles of slow, cautious hiking, we began to hear a rumbling sound coming from somewhere through the trees. It sounded like the crowd noise on a televised football game – the kind that is so loud you can't hear the commentators. As we continued hiking toward the pond the noise became louder until we broke through the trees and skidded to a stop at Dude's Fishing Hole. We were met with a roar that emanated from the horde of people fishing the lake.

Fifteen unsupervised 12-year-old boys that had two fishing rods between them, all yelling for a turn. Families with young children occupying almost every bit of solid ground surrounding the pond and wedged up in the rocks on the far shore, the kids seemingly all crying about something. I guess I never saw the memo stating that today was "Take Your Toddler Fishing Day."

This is no exaggeration: there were at least 100 kids, half of them young enough to be wearing diapers, and 30 adults surrounding this pond that is so small it's hard to see its little blue dot on the map. Don't get me wrong, I love kids and I think fishing is a fantastic way to get them out in the fresh air and away from TV and video games. Just recently we had taken our five-year-old granddaughter fishing in Chaffee County. But after a relatively unpleasant, two-mile hike, the noise and commotion caught me off guard. Where did everyone come from? We climbed back up into the trees a bit and found a log to sit on while we ate our lunch. I pulled out my trail map and studied it more closely. A quarter mile away, in the opposite direction, was the largest campground in the park. *Oh.*

We could still kind of see the pond through the trees, and we could most definitely hear it, so we kept track of the activity around it while we ate our sandwich, hopeful that everyone would suddenly race back to the campground for lunch. But just the opposite happened – more fishing-rod-toting people, most with young kids in tow, kept beating a path to the shore. Kathy asked me if I was going to fish and I told her that I was not. Even if the fish were begging to be caught, there is more to fishing than catching fish, and this sideshow didn't appeal to me. I guess I'm just spoiled from being able to fish in solitude most of the time.

We continued our hike after lunch, heading uphill from the pond on a smooth, wide trail that looked like an interstate highway compared to the path behind us. Once beyond the very popular campground, the trail continued uphill but reverted to its rocky streambed state. Eventually the trail headed downhill again and then undulated for the final half mile to the trailhead. A kid somewhere off in the trees serenaded us the whole way by repeating at the top of his lungs, "Guys, come here, I want to show you something!" *Yeah right. Don't fall for it guys.* It sounded just like my brother when we were kids, hiding around a corner and waiting to ambush me with his dirty socks or underwear.

Once back at the car, it was a relief to take off my pack, which felt like it weighed at least 35 pounds. Despite the very pleasant temperature in the mid-60's I had worked up a pretty good sweat, needlessly hauling that pack over the rocky terrain. Even though it was kind of a crummy hike, we got some good exercise and plenty of fresh, mountain air. When we got back to the house I got on the scale while wearing the backpack and again without it. The difference was 19 pounds. *Really, that's it? What a wimp.*

Campground Serenade

We were back up to the mountain place for the unofficial start of the Aspen-Leaves-Turning-Gold season, or whatever you would like to call it. Perhaps Fall Colors is better. Not as descriptive, but shorter. Typically the third weekend of September is the most colorful, but we were ready for another weekend in Chaffee County so we drove up on the second Saturday.

After settling in and then lunch, I drove upstream a few miles, parking the truck near a popular campground that borders the river. My hope was that the campground would be mostly abandoned now that school was back in session. It *seemed* to be less populated than usual when I walked through it to get to the river. It was an unseasonably warm day, and the typical bright-blue sky was kind of hazy. I waded into the river in my shorts and wet-socks downstream from the campground, crossing over to the far shore, with a grasshopper dry fly and a Rainbow Warrior nymph at the end of my leader. After a couple of casts a trout came to the surface to investigate the hopper, but quickly retreated before I could set the hook. But I had some redemption a few minutes later when a tug on the line, a hook-set and a quick fight brought a decent 12-inch brown to the net. I was a little surprised at how quickly this fish surrendered. I suspect that it had been caught before and decided it would be best to get it over with and pray for release.

Ten minutes later I caught another brown on the nymph, but then I had no further strikes for at least 30 minutes. I decided to change things up a bit so I replaced the hopper with a big, double-bead head Golden Stone, switched the Rainbow Warrior out for a Prince Nymph and added a strike indicator. Before long I was back into fish, catching two more on this rig. But as I worked my way upstream I noticed a lot of activity along the shore at the campground. The low September flow had exposed a beach area where a family of campers were sunbathing and playing in the water. And somewhere in the not-too-distant distance, a dog was barking incessantly. I considered turning back to find another spot to fish, and in retrospect I wish I had.

As I touched on earlier, a large part of the enjoyment I get from fly fishing is the solitude of my surroundings. Generally I am by myself or with a good friend, silently fishing in a mostly quiet world, away from the loud sounds of civilization that invade everyday life. And even when an obnoxiously loud vehicle passes on the nearest road, it is mostly masked by the sound of the rushing water. As it did last weekend at the crowded state park, the tumult across the river today took me by surprise. And it would have been a simple matter to walk downstream, cross the river and drive to another spot to fish. But the river itself looked inviting here. There was some nice structure, good looking seams and tempting pools. So I ignored the fact that the family directly across the river, when not splashing around in the water, was watching me intently.

I fished this area with purpose, confident that hungry trout were plentiful here. But as I slowly worked my way upstream I grew discouraged. I was not getting any strikes and the campground chaos increased considerably. The next sandy area across the river, at a spot that is used as a boat launch for rafts and kayaks during higher water, hosted two or three more families using it as a beach. Kids in swimsuits splashed around on the edge of the water, babies in diapers cried, and one freakishly strong little girl plunged rocks into the water that were almost as big as she was. The adults were gathered around two giant dogs that stood nose-to-nose, barking at each other non-stop in a display of teeth-baring, campground domination. The only way this section of the river could have been louder would be if every jet engine ever built lined the banks and was running at full throttle while every cannon ever produced fired continuously. And yet I continued to fish here because the water just looked so fishy.

I endured the uproar for what seemed like half the day but was probably less than half an hour. At the height of the mayhem, after casting into a v-shaped riffle, my indicator stalled at the end of the drift, and I set the hook. Bam, fish on the line! My rod bent substantially before a nice-sized brownie jumped through the surface, twisting as it went. From across the river I heard a kid's shrill voice pierce the din, "He caught a fish!" Suddenly the world grew quiet, as if a switch had been flipped. The kids stopped splashing, the babies stopped crying, even the dogs stopped barking. I looked across the river long enough to see that everyone had stopped what they were doing and were watching me fight this trout. As if on cue, it jumped through the surface once again, shaking off a spray of water as it arced through the air before splashing down to a chorus of cheers from the campers. Once in the net the kids burst into a round of applause. I looked across the river to see them lined up along the opposite shore clapping and high-fiving each other. I held the 14-inch trout up to show them and when I did their applause actually increased, so what the hell, I took a bow.

After I released the fish, the sonic assault resumed to its pre-fish levels so I quickly fished my way upstream and around the bend. The river here was wide, shallow and very clear. I casted to a few of the most likely spots, but wasn't surprised when no fish came a-callin'. By now I was getting pretty tired. I thought about why that was and decided it was because wading this time of year is more difficult. Even though the water level is low, the rocks on the river-bottom are more slippery because they are under water year-round and therefore covered with algae. Wading when the water is higher has its own challenges due to the faster flow, but the rocks closer to shore are exposed half of the year and therefore aren't coated in slime. This is just my unprofessional opinion. Don't quote me on any of this - I am not a botanist, biologist, or entomologist, although Tucker insists I'm an authority on all things slimy.

I could have waded across the river here to return to the truck and bypass the campground melee, but the bank on the other side was steep and I didn't have the energy to climb it. And besides I wanted to try one more nymph, a green RS2 to hopefully imitate a blue-wing olive emerger. I tied on the new fly and walked back downstream along the rocky shore, occasionally stopping to cast the RS2 upstream. I had no success with this tactic so once I was below the still-raucous campground, to my original starting point, I decided I'd try a dry fly one last time. I re-rigged to fish a single, small BWO, but I had a hard time seeing this fly floating down the river. *If a fish rises near where I think the fly is I'll set the hook and see what happens.* But I didn't have to worry as no fish rose.

Back at the house I fired up the grill and enjoyed a cold beer and a beautiful sunset while cooking a couple of steaks. When I turned away from the setting sun and the grilling steaks I saw the good-sized deer we call Crazy Uncle Buck making his way across the property. The first time we saw Crazy Uncle Buck, a deer we now see around the area frequently, he was acting strangely – like he had a few loose marbles. Maybe it was just the time of year when a young buck's thoughts turn to young does. Since then though he has acted like a normal deer, and this night he sauntered west through the yard before disappearing into the trees and the setting sun.

Creepy Weirdness

The next day Kathy and I decided to get out and explore a little, choosing an area in the southwest part of Chaffee County. Our map showed a county road leading to North Fork Reservoir and further up, Billings Lake. Oh and along the way, if you looked for it apparently you could find a waterfall. But before we left we had a little work to do. Earlier in the week we had purchased an inspection camera that snakes into inaccessible areas, such as inside walls and down heat vents, to let you see what evils may be lurking. We weren't 100 percent certain that we had removed all the dog food in the walls of the house, and we wondered what lay hidden down the heat ducts. So we did our best to feed the slender, stiff, three-foot-long tube into the walls and down the vents, behind the furnace and beneath the water heater in our search for secret caches of mice-hidden dog food. We did not see anything definitive, so we hope that means the problem was isolated to the single wall of the bug room that we had cleaned up two weeks ago.

We then measured how much new insulation we would need to replace what we had removed. While doing that we spotted a doe through the window, lounging in the shade of one of our piñon trees. Kathy went outside to photograph her, after which she made a picnic lunch for our day's venture. (Kathy made the lunch, not the deer.) I loaded my fly gear and Kathy's camera gear into the truck and by the time we stopped for gas and were on the road it was 12:30.

Within a half-hour we were pulling off the highway and onto County Road 240, not too far east of Monarch ski area. The road climbed past a few scattered homes before starting a serpentine course through the trees. After three miles the pavement ended and before long the road narrowed considerably and became rutted and rocky as it followed the North Fork of the South Arkansas River. As we rounded a bend we came upon two ATV's that had stopped and were blocking the narrow trail. The riders were standing next to their ATV's looking down into the creek. When they saw us one guy walked back to where the two of us waited semi-patiently. "There's a fish in that creek!" he said excitedly.

I almost said, "That's a good place for it," but thought better of it and instead said, "Is that right?" trying not to wet myself from excitement.

The guy sensed my lack of enthusiasm and said, "Well, it's kind of cool to see it right from the side of the road."

"Uh-huh. Well, have a good day," I responded, anxious to get this guy and his ATV moving. He got the message and walked kind of dejectedly back to his ATV, pointing at the miracle fish as he went, as if we didn't believe him.

Kathy was curious though, thinking that since this guy had made a big deal of it, perhaps there was a 26-inch

177

cutthroat in this small creek. So she got out of the truck and I followed her to where the guy had been pointing. There was indeed a fish swimming around in a tiny, shallow pool, but it was rather small at about eight inches. We watched it swim around for a moment, and then a few other fish appeared from beneath some deadfall, including one that was decent-sized at about 12 inches. But I didn't for a second consider casting into that narrow stream, buried in the trees as it was and surrounded by dead limbs. I doubted I even had enough room to get my rod out of the tube without getting it caught up in the trees.

We had been keeping track of our mileage on the odometer, knowing that 6.5 miles in was a waterfall supposedly right near the road. As we approached 6.25 miles we began looking and listening for it, but at 6.75 miles, after not spotting any obvious signs, like a sign that said "Waterfall," perhaps in blinking neon, we parked the truck and walked back down the road. We ventured off the trail a time or two, into the dense trees, but found only the flowing brook. Soon enough though we heard the unmistakable sound of rushing water and followed it to where the ground suddenly dropped away, straight down to a narrow, 90-foot-deep ravine. *Jeez, I'd hate to be walking around out here at night.* At the head of this gorge were the picturesque falls, surrounded by scenic rock formations and towering pines. And even though they were difficult to photograph, what with the sheer, instant-death drop-off, we still spent at least 20 minutes here trying to do them justice with our cameras.

We continued our slow journey up the bumpy road toward Billings Lake, bypassing the turn-off to North Fork Reservoir at 10 miles. One mile further up the trail Billings Lake came into view as the trees thinned and the few hearty survivors were noticeably shorter. We bounced our way for the final half mile to the small lake at 12,000 ft., finding it surrounded on three sides by high mountain ridges like so many other lakes in this region. We followed the trail to the far side of the lake where it ended at a locked gate that led to an abandoned mine entrance. I found out later that there is a rare, carved-stone mine entrance near here inscribed with the words "Pride of the West Tunnel 1880."

We parked the truck at a small parking area in front of the gate, where one other vehicle was parked. There was a guy at the tailgate that looked to be gearing up to fish, so I walked over to make small talk. "Are there fish in this lake?" I asked.

"I aim to find out pretty quick. I thought I could see some rising out toward the center."

There was a woman sitting in the front passenger seat with her window cracked, so Kathy said hello to her while I was talking to the guy. Kathy and I then walked a couple of dozen feet to the water's edge to see what we could see. The lake was heavy with underwater vegetation and combined with the cold wind that began blowing I decided I was just asking for trouble if I fished here. We couldn't help but notice a canoe along the shore that presumably belonged to Tailgate Guy, who seemed to be taking an awful long time rigging up his spinning rod. We walked back to the truck and before departing said goodbye to Mr. and Mrs. Tailgate Guy. That's when I realized that he was indeed stalling – just waiting for us to leave.

As we drove away, I said to Kathy, "That was kind of weird."

"Yeah, and did you see that other guy sitting in the back seat?"

"No, really?"

"Yeah, he looked like he was trying not to be seen."

"Wow, that's creepy."

We drove back toward the trail that headed down the mountain, but within a few minutes found a campsite that overlooked the lake and decided to stop and eat our lunch. While we did I pulled out the map and noticed that just on the other side of the high ridge to the north was Pomeroy Lakes, and on the other side of the western ridge was Hancock Lakes, both occasional fishing destinations of mine.

After a few minutes of sandwich-eating and map-reading we saw Tailgate Guy and one other person glide across the lake in the canoe. Tailgate Guy sat up front and fished while the other person, either Mrs. Tailgate Guy or Shadowy Backseat Dude, rowed to where Tailgate Guy pointed. And when the rower wasn't rowing he/she sat motionless, leaning forward in a submissive posture and looking down into the canoe while Tailgate Guy fished. Creepy weird.

Bouncing our way back down the mountainside, we turned off on the spur road that led to North Fork Reservoir and the small, adjacent campground. We passed a few people camping at casual spots before getting to the "official" Forest Service campground. Once there we saw a notice posted at the self-pay station indicating that the campground was closed due to overflowing vault toilets. Yuck. I presume they couldn't get the toilet-sucking truck up the "crappy" road. We had to circle through the little campground to get to the lake and found it empty and eerily quiet, like it had been closed for some time. The reservoir itself was surrounded by beautiful trees with scraggy mountain peaks rising above it to the west, and was surprisingly large considering its remote location. It too was very quiet – we didn't see a single person around the lake.

For some reason I wasn't tempted to fish. Perhaps because I've never really had much luck in bigger lakes, or maybe I was just a little burned out from my strange day of fishing yesterday. If I *had* fished here it certainly would have been more serene than yesterday. We drove slowly back down the bone-jarring trail 10 miles to the highway and then another 12 miles to downtown Salida, where a wood-fired pizza and a cold microbrew were a welcome end to our day.

Dead Tree Blues

It was now unofficially the prime fall-colors weekend in Chaffee County. To celebrate the third-September weekend, the first thing I did after our mid-Saturday-morning arrival was to go the hardware store. I bought some fuel stabilizer for the lawnmower since I wasn't planning to use it again until next summer. So that was exciting. The action continued after lunch when I sprayed foam insulation into any crevice I could find inside the bare wall of the bug room in an attempt to slow the mice through their super-highway.

By two o'clock I was at the river, deciding to once again fish the apparently public water south of the campground that I had discovered just a month earlier. After traversing the campground and crossing the river I walked downstream along the shore for at least a half-hour until I came upon the no-trespassing sign nailed to the tree. I stopped here and began fishing my way back upstream the way I had came.

I started with a good-sized, rubber-legged terrestrial pattern as my top fly, with a small Green Drake nymph tagging along beneath the surface. Being cautious of a large fallen tree that sprawled across the tail end of a deep pool, I casted in. After a couple of casts a fish rose to the dry fly but I missed the strike. After the next cast, as my flies drifted through the pool, I scanned the river in search of a good spot for the following cast. Unfortunately I didn't pay enough attention to my drifting flies and when I attempted to pick them up and recast they were caught in the deadfall. *Crud. Really?* I waded over to the fallen tree as the river bottom fell away beneath my feet. After some maneuvering to avoid the deepest spots I managed to sidle up next to the tree while standing waist deep in fairly swift current. I felt around underwater among the branches for a few minutes and discovered that my leader was wrapped nastily around the submerged limbs. *Crap.*

Now I imagine at this point most fishermen would cut their leader at the lowest, accessible spot, climb out of the rushing water and spend a couple of minutes to re-rig. But as you have undoubtedly realized by now, I am not like most fishermen. For one thing, it takes me more than a few minutes to tie on tippet and new flies. For another, I hate to lose flies. Leaving those flies there would have been like nailing a $5 bill to that tree. Plus there's the principal of the thing: these are my flies, not the trees, and I want them back. So I stood waist-deep in the cold, forceful water, on slippery rocks, enveloped in dead-tree limbs. For at least 10 minutes I attempted to unwrap my flies from the clutches of the wicked tree with one hand while trying to maintain control of my rod with the other, and not get the free part of my line caught up in the branches. I finally managed to liberate my flies and escape unscathed, quickly scampering upriver to distance myself from the fly-eating tree.

After a few more casts I caught a brown trout on the Green Drake, which made me forget my dead-tree blues. And in short order, after missing a dry-fly strike, I hooked and netted a nice-sized rainbow that surfaced for the terrestrial. As I released it, I realized that it was the first rainbow I had caught in quite some time. When I mentioned this to Todd later he said that he hadn't caught many rainbows this year either. After fishing my way slowly upstream for an hour I saw another No-Trespassing sign nailed to a tree – a sign I had missed on my way downstream. *Crap!* Without realizing it I had been trespassing for an hour. My apologies to the landowner. If he ever wants to spend an hour walking around on my weed and cactus-choked lot he is more than welcome.

I did catch another, smaller rainbow later in the day, along with a few more browns. The final tally for the afternoon was seven fish in the net, about that many missed dry-fly strikes, and about that many that weaseled free after being hooked. Not to mention the large rainbow that spit out the fly as it was cart-wheeling through the air four feet above the surface.

As I walked through the quiet campground on my way back to the truck I came across a camper tending his fire.

"How's it going?" I asked. "Didn't I see you here last weekend?"

"Yeah, I've been camping here all week. It's beautiful here."

It sure is, I thought, as the autumn sunset glowed pink behind the golden peaks. "Where are you from?"

"Wichita. I drove out for my vacation. Having a great time."

We spoke for a few more minutes, mostly about fishing the river. As I continued on to the truck I thought about how fortunate I am to have a house, as modest as it is, just a few minutes down the road from a place that people gladly drive nine hours from Wichita to experience.

Lumpy Rutherford

Since the third weekend of September has typically been a beautiful time for fall colors in the region we were anxious to get out for some photography. We discussed going to several tried-and-true areas we had photographed in the past, but instead decided that we wanted to explore somewhere new. According to a guide book we have, west of Leadville is a relatively easy 4-wheel-drive route called Hagerman Pass that has some historical interest as it loosely follows an old railroad route, and is colorful in the fall. As it turned out it was not easy, colorful or particularly interesting. So thanks a lot, Guide-Book Guy.

We drove north to Leadville and then west over the Turquoise Lake dam. The road climbed the hillside skirting the south and west sides of the lake, offering an occasional glimpse of the lake through the pines. When we came to a fork in the road we heeded Yogi Berra's advice and took it. The left fork was a dirt road that climbed away from the lake and headed south. After a couple of miles down the washboard road we came to a huge dirt opening among the trees at around 10,850 feet elevation that apparently was the staging area for the construction of the 1.8 mile long Busk-Ivanhoe tunnel. Completed in 1891 to carry train traffic through the mountain beneath the Continental Divide, it was later used for automobiles and then as a conduit for water, which still flows through it before coursing its way to Turquoise Lake. There were a few vehicles parked in this giant dirt patch, so we got out to see what the attraction was. We wandered around a bit, seeing the sealed opening to the tunnel before discovering the sign indicating this was the trailhead for the 1.6 mile hike to Windsor Lake.

Back in the truck, the road suddenly became much worse and we slowed to a crawl as we bounced rudely over the now ubiquitous rocks. (Note to self: form a rock band and call it Ubiquitous Rocks.) Kathy's white-knuckle gripping of the armrest was a not-too-subtle hint that I had better not steer too close to the steep drop-off on the passenger side. The road smoothed a bit before long and through an opening in the trees we saw Turquoise Lake once again, this time from high above it. We gladly got out of the truck to give our internal organs a break from the jarring ride and to photograph the lake. For the rest of our trip the road surface varied between bumpy-as-hell to spleen-bursting insanity. (Note to self: when Ubiquitous Rocks breaks up, call the next band Spleen-Bursting Insanity.) If they named roads after TV characters, this one would be called Lumpy Rutherford. But we drove on in our quest for the quintessential Colorado-golden-aspen photograph.

After our photography stop the road snaked further away from the lake and before long climbed above tree line. We stopped on a rocky, windswept ridge to photograph a much smaller body of water called Hagerman Lake, deposited in a glacial cirque far below where we stood at 11,500 ft. From here it was a short, bouncy drive to the summit of the pass, where it straddles the Continental Divide at 11,925 ft. We stopped for the obligatory photos with the sign and considered turning around here. We hadn't seen the profusion of autumn gold that was promised by the guide book, so we considered cutting our losses and driving back down to make the hike to Windsor Lake. But instead we continued on, hopeful that the road would be smoother and the aspen more plentiful on the west side of the pass. Unfortunately it was not to be.

Don't get me wrong, with the exception of a few places, including one where we spun the wheels of the 4x4 before gaining traction on a precarious perch, the road was not technically difficult to drive. I never worried about damaging the vehicle like when travelling to Pomeroy or Hancock Lakes. It was just extremely rough, making for a slow, uncomfortable trip.

As we inched our way down toward timberline on the Pacific side of the divide a good-sized body of water came into view. We stopped to look at the map and saw that this was Ivanhoe Lake. We snaked slowly on, eventually stopping along the road just below timberline at a vantage point well above the 11,000 ft. lake. Finally seeing fall color, mostly from low-lying vegetation, we framed the lake in the mid-ground, with the high mountain peaks in the distance and the golden foliage in the foreground. We got some decent photos, but was it worth the effort and discomfort? Hell no! I complained to Kathy that I had only seen six aspen trees in three hours. While I may have been exaggerating, (which is a fisherman's obligation) I wasn't exaggerating by much.

After our photo session we hopped back in the truck and sat eating our sandwiches while enjoying the view. It really was beautiful and it was nice to be there off the beaten path. I just felt misled by the book that promised an easy drive and an explosion of fall colors. After lunch we made a 16-point turn on the narrow pathway and headed back uphill the way we had come. The road was no better heading the opposite direction, but by 3 p.m. we had traversed the pass once again before pulling up in one piece at the Windsor Lake trailhead, back down at 10,850 feet.

"Do you want to hike to the lake?" I asked. "It's supposed to be 1.6 miles."

"Sure," said Kathy, always ready for some high-elevation exercise. We had no idea what we were in for.

I loaded our gear into my daypack, including my fly rod, and we crossed the water that flowed out of the Busk-Ivanhoe tunnel. We followed the trail as it meandered pleasantly through the trees for a few hundred feet. That would be the last time the word "pleasant" would enter my mind for the next hour. Without warning the trail began a steep ascent. For a little while it continued to curve around a bit, as if trying to convince us it wasn't really that steep. But we were not fooled, our unwilling legs and burning lungs revealing the truth. Soon the trail gave up all pretenses of pleasantness and began to climb straight uphill. No turns, no switchbacks, nothing to help ease the climb. We turned sideways to sidestep up the steep, gravelly incline, reaching out for bushes, rocks, tree limbs – anything to grasp to pull ourselves up the hill.

Whenever we reached a rare patch of flat ground we stopped to catch our breath, spending twice as long standing still as we did moving. When we came to a spot along the trail where there was nothing to pull ourselves up with, we made our own little mini-switchbacks. Like when we were kids with one-speed bikes riding up a steep hill and would zigzag from side-to-side to try to gain some uphill momentum. Except now, instead of a paved, thirty foot wide street, we would zig 14 inches across the steep, dirt slope before zagging back 14 inches, with a net elevation gain of perhaps four inches. *This is ridiculous.*

While resting at a flat spot in front of a cave entrance, too exhausted to be curious about the cave or even concerned that a ferocious beast could come thundering out of it at any second, we seriously discussed turning back.

"I saw a mountain goat slip and fall back there," I told Kathy.

"Oh, you did not."

"I'm serious. And did you see that giant pile of bones? It was from all the pack-burros that have perished trying to climb this hill."

She paused before asking me, "Do you want to go back?"

I paused even longer before responding, "No, surely the trail is going to get better."

The trail did eventually get better, but not before continuing its course straight up and nearly killing us. But it finally leveled off slightly and even wound around a few trees. It was through those trees, an hour after we began our climb, that we caught our first glimpse of the lake. A heavenly light shone down on it and the angels began to sing, easing our burden and beckoning us to its shores. Or maybe this damn trail had killed me after all and this was heaven. It looked like it could be. So we kept walking, almost with a spring in our step, as we entered the level clearing that held the small lake at 11,600 feet.

The lake very scenically sat in a mountain meadow surrounded by rugged peaks. And there wasn't another person anywhere within sight or earshot. But it wasn't very big and it looked really shallow. I was anxious to see if it held fish, but Kathy asked me to wait before I started wandering its shores. She wanted to get a few unobstructed photos before I could gunk them up. I sat anxiously on a rock for ten minutes waiting for Kathy, nervous the whole time that people and splashing dogs would come along and scare whatever fish may be in this very clear water.

When I got the green light from Kathy I crossed the soggy glade to the nearby lake outlet, crouching down low and going into ninja mode as I got closer. But when I was about 15 feet away I still managed to startle a fish. It bolted out of the narrow outflow stream and into the lake, sending out an alarm to its buddies as it went. *Crap. Well, at least I know there are fish in there. Maybe by the time I've rigged my rod they will have forgotten about me.* I backed off a couple of dozen yards and kneeled down in the tall, wet grass to assemble my rod and tie on a fly. As I was doing this a group of three or four hikers appeared in the meadow and dropped their gear, obviously spent from their climb up. I hadn't made a single cast and the party could be over. But after a few photographs, presumably with me floundering around in the middle, they continued up the trail and out of sight. *Hmm, I wonder where the trail goes from here.*

Once ready, I crept over to the outlet again and after a couple of attempts I managed to land my fly, a small Blue Wing Olive adult, in the narrow stream. No sign of life. After several more casts without a response I casted into the lake proper, right in front of the outlet. Still nothing. I worked my way quickly around a quarter of the small lake without seeing a fish until I came to a particularly clear, shallow area where I spotted dozens of them swimming about. When my fly hit the water in their midst they all scattered. But one or two came back to investigate before swimming off again. After repeating this routine for about five minutes a fish finally took a chance and ate the fly. I set the hook and the fish reacted as if it were on fire. It swam around so erratically that I was afraid it would kill itself within 30 seconds. So I gave it as much slack as I could, but it was extremely resistant to any attempt I made to bring it to the shore.

Eventually I got the thing to the bank, but since I had elected not to bring the net along on the hike, and since the fish was less than cooperative, I had to step into the lake in my hiking boots to secure it. When the damn thing stopped wiggling I saw that I had a beautiful cutthroat, quite possibly a greenback. It was about 10 inches long, and what it lacked in size it made up for in feistiness. Unfortunately the fly was about a half mile down its gullet, and my lack of net and the jiggling fish made it difficult to remove the fly. When I finally got the fly out, now coated with fish blood, I spent about 45 seconds reviving the fish before it squirmed free. But it only swam 12 inches before it stopped to rest for what seemed like an extended time. So I reached back in, easily grabbed the fish and started more vigorous revival. I held the fish tighter this time and did not let go until a strong tail-flip propelled it out of my hand and back to join its buddies.

Having been warned by the bloody-mouthed cutthroat, the rest of the fish in this area would have nothing to do with my fly. So I walked around to the inlet of the lake and found even more fish here. This time not a single fish showed any interest at all in my offering. They were mostly facing the inlet, feeding on whatever was flowing into the lake, and like a bonehead I was standing at the inlet where they all could see me through the clear, shallow water as I waved my rod around. I changed my fly, like that would somehow help, but of course it didn't.

After an hour at the lake it was 5 p.m. and time to head back down the ridiculously steep trail before it got dark. We picked our way down slowly and after about a quarter mile we were overtaken by a younger couple, both carrying fly rods. The guy asked me if I had any luck and I told him about the single cutthroat. He then pulled out his phone and showed me a picture of an 18-inch cutthroat he had just caught. There definitely was no one else fishing at the lake while I was there, so I asked him, "Where were you fishing?"

"Windsor Lake," he replied.

"Oh, I didn't see you there."

"Were you fishing at the pond?" he asked.

"Wait a second, what?"

"Yeah, Windsor Lake is about a hundred yards around the bend from that first little pond you come to."

"Seriously?" I asked, in a combination of bewilderment and disgust. "Crap!" We had almost killed ourselves only to stop 300 feet short of our destination.

Fish, Beer and Cheerleaders

Todd and Laurie came up to our mountain place on the first Friday night of October, with me and Kathy making the drive on our now-customary Saturday morning. We hauled some old carpet up with us to put in the bug room as a temporary measure, hopeful that we have solved the carpet-beetle problem. We didn't yet want to buy new carpet and officially install it until we knew for sure that the bugs would not return. So when our Denver-neighbor Jack offered up his lightly-used dining room carpet, which is in much better shape than anything we own, we jumped at it. Todd helped me unload it, and then the four of us fed it through the window and into the bug room.

Based on my tales of relative success, Todd was anxious to fish the spot along the river I had fished the last time out, so after a quick sandwich we headed upstream. We parked the truck 10 minutes from the house, and walked back downstream for 15 or 20 minutes before coming to the first No Trespassing sign we saw – the one I had missed last week. Based on the recommendation of the fly-shop guy, I tied on three flies – a big foam hopper, a good-sized Copper John and a small Barr's Emerger. My first and only other attempt at fishing three flies ended almost immediately in a massive tangle thanks to my herky-jerky casting motion. When I told the fly shop guy this, his advice was, "Don't cast herky-jerky." *Um, thanks.*

When I told Todd the guy's recommendation Todd said, "I almost always fish with three flies. And so on this day I tried the three-fly setup and all went well - for about 15 minutes.

In those first 15 minutes I caught two trout – an 11-inch brown and a 12-inch rainbow. I didn't see Todd catch any fish so I was feeling kind of cocky, until he walked upstream to where I was standing knee-deep in the river. "How's it going?" I asked, anxious to tell him of my success.

"Good, I caught three so far. How about you?"

Crap. "Two."

"Great! This is a beautiful stretch of river," he said over his shoulder as he moved upstream past me. At that moment my day went downhill in a hurry.

True to form, I began my usual routine of massive tangles. It seemed like every cast had the same result – flies wrapped around flies with the whole freakin' glob wrapped around my fly rod. But each time I very patiently untangled the whole mess, determined to master the three-fly technique. Alright let's be honest, I am not going to master anything when it comes to fly fishing. But perhaps I could at least not suck at it so bad. So I kept at it, occasionally getting off a decent cast and drift. But over the next two hours I only caught one more fish. Much of this had to do with the fish not being interested in eating a tangled blob of flies, leader and tippet floating through their feeding lane. Spending more time untangling twisted knots than actually fishing didn't help either. But on the occasions when I actually had a smooth cast into likely water, followed by a good drift, I was still not catching fish. I think this is where my Fly-Fishing Theory of Sloppy Seconds (FFTSS) comes into play.

Todd fishes his way upstream much faster than I do. Even when I'm not untangling knots, retrieving my flies from tree branches or taking forever to tie on a different fly with my fumbling, pudgy fingers, I fish very methodically, trying to cover practically every square inch of likely water. And if there is a particular place I am trying to land a fly, I'll keep casting there until I hit it. Particularly if I'm not catching fish and I resign myself to "practice." So when Todd and I fish together it is not long before he overtakes me as he fishes his way upstream. This leaves me fishing water that he has just recently fished. Some days he will walk back downstream to see what the hell is taking me so long, as he did this day.

"How's it going?" he asked me.

"Kinda crappy."

"How come?"

"I've only caught one more fish, and these tangles are driving me crazy."

"Jeez, really? I've caught 20."

Thanks for rubbing it in, I thought. But I said, "That's great! What are they taking?"

"Just about everything I try. I've caught a ton on this Prince Nymph. Here try one."

He handed me a black Prince Nymph from his fly box and I promptly dropped it among the rocks of the shore, never to be seen again. "Crap. I think I have one of these - I'll tie it on." But when Todd walked back upstream, I immediately tied on something completely different, thinking (probably incorrectly) that the fish I was encountering were wary of Todd's black Prince Nymph by now. I also gave up on the three-fly rig.

I tied on a big, hairy dry fly and a single bright-red nymph below that, thinking that I would rather not be catching fish than dealing with human-head-sized tangles.

And immediately I was confidently casting smooth and tangle-free, while keeping a keen eye on the dry fly for the subtle dip that indicated a quiet nibble on the nymph below the surface. I was startled when a big rainbow suddenly emerged with a crash and swallowed the dry fly! But despite my surprise I managed to hook and land the beautiful 14-incher, telling it upon release, "A little Tylenol should ease the stinging sensation in your lip."

Suddenly, now that the sun had gone behind the mountain and darkness was rapidly descending, my day got a whole lot better. That one fish turned a day of frustration into a learning experience (don't try a three-fly rig again for a long, long time) and made me realize what a beautiful day in a beautiful setting it had been. Fishing my way upstream, I could see Todd up ahead, fishing at our cross-back-over-the-river-to-the-truck spot while waiting for me. I picked up my pace, walking upstream and casting in occasionally as I went. I stopped at a nice-looking pool fed by a rippling current and casted in a few times, but it was getting hard to see the fly in the twilight. *Alright, one final cast.* Bam! I didn't see it as much as I felt it, an unmistakable tug on the line. I set the hook and felt an angry series of short pulls in response. The fish put up a valiant effort, but before long the 12-inch brownie was in my net. I sent him on his way with some advice: "Does that bright-red fly really look like something you should be eating?"

Upon meeting up with Todd I told him I had switched to two flies and caught two more fish. Todd said he caught a total of 24 for the day. I can't imagine catching 24 fish in one day. Perhaps it would be like scoring with every cheerleader on the squad in one night. Another thing that I thought would never happen: when we got back to the house the refrigerator held cold beer that was actually purchased by Todd. *Well, I'll be damned.* Maybe the 24 fish/every cheerleader thing is possible after all.

Name This Story and Win $1,000! Disclaimer: Not Really. But Feel Free to Call It Whatever You Want

After breakfast on Sunday Todd helped me take the swamp cooler out of the den window and stash it in a bedroom closest. We had left it in all last winter but we were constantly fighting drafts that blew in around it, plus I had to replace the float valve come summer.

Kathy and Laurie were anxious to hike on what was shaping up to be a beautiful, fall day. Laurie suggested several hikes in the Monarch Pass area and before long we were out the door, without having decided which hike to take. Todd and I loaded our fishing gear in the truck "just in case." One of the hikes was the Fooses Creek Trail, which just happened to start at Fooses Lake, which supposedly held a healthy trout population. I voted for that option, reasoning that we could have our cake and eat it too - the women could hike and the men could fish. Everyone was agreeable and within 40 minutes we were piling out of the truck into the cool autumn air at the 8,950 ft. Fooses Lake.

It is a small lake, no bigger really than the pond we mistook for Windsor Lake two weeks ago, although deeper. Before gearing up for fishing and hiking we walked a few yards to the shoreline and saw rings scattered across the lake's surface indicating rising fish. Todd had suggested during the drive that if the lake didn't look very fishy we could hike with the women instead, but now that the fish were rising he hurriedly got his fly gear together without further discussion. I followed suit and before long the women had disappeared up the trail and Todd and I were standing along the lakeshore wondering what fly to use.

I decided to tie on a smallish, rubber-legged terrestrial with a red Copper John dangling below that. Since there was a lot of vegetation ringing the lake – aspen trees, cottonwoods, evergreens and willows - I waded in a few feet in order to cast perpendicular to the shore and hopefully not snag anything on my backcast. The water was quite calm and clear enough when the sun was out that I could see fish swimming around by the dozens. After my first several casts were totally ignored by the resident subsurface population, I decided to change flies. This time I tied on a big Parachute Adams and a much smaller Parachute Adams trailing 20 inches or so behind. I hoped that the big fly would act as an indicator to the small fly and also bring curious fish to investigate before settling for the small one. I moved to another spot along the lake, figuring that the fish at the first spot were on to me by now.

I casted in just a couple of times before deciding that the gigantic Parachute Adams looked ridiculous floating around out there, so I decided to cast it in just once more before changing flies again. And of course on the next backcast the damn thing got snagged 30 feet up in a tree. After trying unsuccessfully to free it I finally had to resort to the old give-it-a-big-yank trick which produced the expected result of a broken tippet knot, leaving my two flies dangling from the tree top. *There's five bucks down the drain.*

This time I chose a much smaller white-colored dry as my top fly, trailed by an even smaller, brownish-green dry fly with a little flash. When I casted this set-up into the lake I could see the fish come over to have a look, occasionally turning back for a second look after their first refusal. I figured that it was only a matter of time before one of them took a chance. And I enjoyed being able to see far enough below the surface to watch how the fish reacted to my flies instead of the rolling-river routine of staring at just the fly and waiting for a sudden fish emergence. Before long I tried giving the fly a little life by jiggling the rod tip or giving the line a very short, quick strip in an attempt to solicit a strike. And what do you know, a fish that had swam over to have a look, swam off, swam back and then off again, turned around when I jiggled the fly and decided to have a bite. Since I could see everything so clearly I was able to lift the rod tip at the right time and hook it. It put up a jumping, splashy fight but came to the net in due course - an 11-inch brown trout with a disappointed look in its eye.

I moved a few yards away, just on the other side of a big pine tree and casted again. A few moments later I watched as a fair-sized fish came over to check out my flies. Without hesitation it pounced on the smaller fly and again with a perfect view of the action I was able to set the hook. The noisy reluctance of this trout to swim into my net caught Todd's attention, who left his perch at the small dam to come have a look. By the time he got there I had netted a 14-inch rainbow, which Todd duly photographed with me before I released it. Todd asked which fly had done the job and I showed it to him, although by now it was mangled pretty much beyond recognition.

I switched out the chewed-up fly for something similar and while I was at it I switched the top fly for something smaller as well, since I was having no trouble seeing the small flies on the calm water. Todd went to a similar rig and almost immediately caught a brown followed by a rainbow. I walked about 50 feet closer to the dam and caught another nice-sized rainbow. After trying the area in front of the lake outlet for a few minutes, where the water flowed over the small spillway, I moved around to the other side of the lake. Earlier I had noticed a few mountain-bikers speed down the path that parallels this side of the lake, but now that I was fishing just a few feet from the trail there was a torrent of them, complete with fancy helmets and team jerseys. I began to worry about hooking one of them with a backcast as they cruised silently out of the trees.

The sun suddenly disappeared behind the clouds and the wind picked up, making it impossible to peer beneath the choppy surface and difficult to see the small dry flies bouncing on the now-dark lake. But after a few more casts I managed to hook and net another decent rainbow, although it wasn't as much fun as it was when I could see the fish cautiously approaching.

I continued to another spot further around, now fishing almost directly across the small lake from Todd, who by now had circumnavigated the lake and was back at our original starting point. After a few casts I considered heading back to that side, thinking that perhaps I could get a better angle to see below the surface and wouldn't have to worry about foul-hooking a mountain-biker. But just then Kathy and Laurie returned from their hike, the wind blew harder and it started to rain. *Seems like a good time to call it a day.* The three of us headed for the truck while Todd endured the elements. About the time we had geared down and settled into our seats

Todd appeared and hurriedly put his gear in the back as the rain intensified.

After we had driven a few hundred feet down the dirt road Todd suddenly cried out, "Crap, stop the truck! I left my rod on the roof!"

I quickly checked the rear-view mirror to see a mountain-biker impatiently careening down the road just inches from our bumper. If I hit the brakes now, this guy would no doubt slam into the back of us, go hurtling over the roof and land on the hood. So I pulled over to one side as far as possible to let the bicyclist by and eased to a stop, trying to keep Todd's $1200 rod and reel from sliding off the roof and into the ditch.

"And there it goes," Todd said calmly as he watched it fall, presumably in slow motion, past his window. When he got out to retrieve it however, he began to call himself names. "Dumbass, what the hell's the matter with you?"

It looked to me like the rod had landed softly in a bed of leaves along the roadside. Plus I knew from my own experience with my much cheaper rod that if Todd's rod was broken it would be repaired by the manufacturer for a minimal charge under the lifetime warranty.

But Todd continued to berate himself as he picked up his rod. "You must be some kind of moron to do that, #$@&%!" He opened up the back hatch to put the rod in. "Well, it *looks* OK. But it could have some hairline cracks. I wonder if I can have it x-rayed?" he said with all seriousness.

In a few minutes we were back on the highway, driving in and out of the rain. When I sensed Todd had calmed down a bit I asked him how many fish he wound up catching. "Two," he said solemnly.

"You mean I actually caught more than you did?" I asked incredulously, trying not to let my voice betray my joy.

"You've out-fished me before," Todd replied matter-of-factly.

"Not that I recall, but I've had some pretty good dreams about it."

Back at the house the sky was clear and the ground was dry, obviously not having rained here. Todd and Laurie packed their car for the return trip to Denver, courteously cleaned the bedroom and bathroom they had used and bid us farewell. An hour later, while I was cutting replacement insulation for the bug room, Laurie texted to say that traffic was at a standstill near the village of Jefferson, apparently due to an accident. I certainly wasn't having any fun cutting insulation, but I was sure glad I wasn't caught up in the traffic. A few minutes later I changed my mind.

As I knelt down to one knee to trim the insulation around an electrical outlet, I somehow managed to instead slam my knee into the metal bed frame. An intense pain shot down my leg and I immediately began screaming obscenities that would have made a drunken pirate blush. I was certain that when I had enough courage to look down at my leg the bottom half would be severed off, laying there in a bloody pool next to the bed. Kathy came running into the room and was relieved to see that I was all in one piece, but also confused why I was screaming so much without having lost any limbs. She quickly got me some ice and when I rolled up my jeans to apply it I expected the knee cap to at least be sheared off. What I saw instead was just a slight hint of a scratch. *That's weird. OK, well, it's probably gonna swell up like a hot-air balloon in a few minutes and then they'll have to amputate.*

After icing it for 15 or 20 minutes it felt good enough to get back to the insulation work. I iced it frequently over the next few days and it never did swell up or fall off, although I had the strange sensation that the leg was several inches shorter than my other one and I limped around like a three-legged jackass for the better part of a week.

Second-Hand Carpet and Pissed-Off Bears

Two weeks later we pulled up to the mountain house at 1:30 p.m. on a mid-October Friday, after a drive that took 20 minutes longer than usual. There seemed to be a lot of slow-moving vehicles along the way - mostly campers pulling ATVs, which I assumed, based on the time of year, were being driven by hunters. A construction delay in Trout Creek Gorge, where they appear to be widening the highway, added to our travel time. Our first order of business was to deal with a mouse caught in a trap. It was disappointing to know we still have mice, but encouraging that our traps are working. Besides, maybe this was the bastard responsible for filling our walls with dog food.

We then moved all the furniture out of the bug room, laid out Jack's carpet that we had brought up last time, and very inexpertly cut it to sorta fit. While Kathy vacuumed up all the chunks from the butchered carpet I ran over to the fly shop. The last time out my relatively new tape-measure zinger broke, my fluorocarbon tippet ran out and my dull nippers that don't so much nip as they do gnaw finally frustrated me enough to want to replace them. After making my purchase and visiting with the fly-shop guy a few minutes, I returned to the house to learn from Kathy that I hadn't cut out the carpet for the heat vent. *Oops.*

It was a beautiful day - calm and sunny - and there was still about 1-1/2 hours of daylight remaining, so I decided to fish. By the time I geared up, drove two miles upstream and walked to the river it was close to 5:30 – maybe an hour of daylight left. I tied on a big Golden Stonefly and a very small, grey RS2 and after a few casts I caught a small brownie. 10 minutes later my indicator dipped again, but this time the fish felt substantially stronger. I didn't rush it to the net, but once there I saw that I had landed a hefty, 14-inch trout, another brown.

I fished for another 45 minutes without a strike before it became too dark too see what I was doing. I pulled the bear-spray out of my pocket and held onto it while walking to the truck through the piñon trees in the gathering darkness. I figured this time of year the bears are consuming mega-calories for the upcoming winter's nap, and a skinny-legged dork that smells of fish may be irresistible to any bear I may encounter. Although what I carry isn't officially bear spray but a small "personal protection" canister of Mace. Because I'm too cheap to buy the full-blown bear spray, and the canisters are just too darn big to carry conveniently. So one of these days, if I do get threatened by a bear, I'll probably just piss it off enough with my Mace that when the can quickly runs dry the bear will have a legitimate excuse to eat me. (Yet another legal disclaimer: I don't really know what I'm talking about here. I'm sure Mace is a fine product if used as intended.)

Memories...Like the Hum, Hum, Something, Something

The fall weather had been incredibly mild, but it could turn cold any time now. So on Saturday morning I decided it was time to replace the bug and mouse-crap infested insulation I had removed from the crawl space in May. Forgetting my hard hat back in Denver, I donned a purple bike helmet and the N95 respirator, crawled into the subterranean hantavirus breeding ground, strung out the fire-hazard work lights and took measurements for the insulation. Returning above ground to fresh air I cut all the insulation and then brought the pieces back down into the crawl space for placement between the studs. Despite the fact that a massive metal support beam runs the length of the house just 18 inches in front of the wall where I was working, I only conked my head 4,016 times.

After lunch I headed for the west side of the river, directly across from where I fished last night. On my walk from the truck to the river channel I came across elk tracks and droppings, which is notable because I've never seen elk near the river. I see them in the fields occasionally, but they aren't as ubiquitous around here as deer, which are all over the place, including in the yard. I fished for at least 45 minutes without any action, changing flies frequently in hopes of finding something the fish would be interested in. Finally a tiny brown, maybe seven or eight inches, hit a small, flashy, bright red nymph. I was disappointed in the size of the fish, but maybe I finally found a fly that would work.

But still the fishing was very slow until another fish, this one much bigger, struck about half an hour later. But I was too anxious to land it and it broke free, taking with it both my top and bottom flies. *Damn!* Not too long after that I hooked another good-sized fish and after what I thought was a successful fight, it suddenly flipped up into the air as I was coaxing it into the net, threw the fly and swam off. *Come on already!*

I continued upstream for the next hour and a half, still switching flies with regularity, without any indication that there was a fish within a hundred miles. And my frequent companion – tangles - came to visit once again. Despite this, I decided to complicate my casting further by adding weight to my line. When the weight stays where I put it, my tangles increase exponentially in frequency and tonnage. But often times the weight does not stay put, either flying off on a cast or getting wedged between rocks, where it stays when I jerk the line out of frustration. And my small, football-shaped indicators also kept flying off. It was as if I was being told just to stop. Go home, you suck.

But of course I didn't stop. *Quit being such a doofus and figure this out!* I tied on a double bead-head Golden Stonefly with a very small BWO emerger. This set-up is what I had unsuccessfully started with today, but it had produced fair results yesterday. I cast it into the top of a cascade and let it follow the flow into a large pool. At the top of the pool the indicator stalled ever so slightly. I thought the bottom fly had probably just snagged momentarily on a rock, but I lifted the rod tip in case I was wrong. I felt a thick, quivering resistance and watched my indicator rocket downstream as the hooked fish barreled toward the tail end of the pool like a freight train. It was bolting for the safety of a submerged log and I had to work to keep it from burrowing beneath it, while trying not to put too much pressure on this energetic fish. It did swim back upstream and away from the log before moving out into the main flow, which it followed downstream and into the next pool. I hurriedly pursued it, splashing out of the pool before stumbling my way along the rocky shore, all while trying to keep just the right amount of tension on the line. When I reached the downstream pool the fish greeted me with an aerial show of acrobatics. The first time it jumped through the surface I could see it was a good-sized fish. The second time, the golden afternoon light slanting through the trees revealed that it was a colorful rainbow trout. The third time I just enjoyed the moment: a big, brightly-colored rainbow twisting and flipping through the air on a beautiful fall day in the Rocky Mountains.

Finally, after perhaps ten minutes, the rainbow seemed ready to come to the net. But at the last moment, for the second time today, the fish turned, jumped into the air, flipped and spun in a last ditch attempt to escape. I didn't let my guard down this time though, and managed to keep it on the line. Admitting defeat, it finally allowed itself to be netted. I marveled at how colorful this fish was – an iridescent greenish-silver with a very pronounced bright-pink stripe. When I attempted to retrieve it from the net to remove the fly I was impressed by its weight and girth. But ever the rebel, the fish wanted no part in being handled by the likes of me, so I put it back in the net and easily took out the fly while it laid there. It did let me pick it up to release it however, and although it was still feisty and appeared strong, I hung onto it under water for several moments until a convincing tail thrash sent it cruising away.

If I was smart I would have ended my fishing day right then on that high note. But as you undoubtedly know by now, I'm not that smart. A decent breeze had started blowing straight upstream, further complicating my already suspect casting. Finally, after another half-hour of losing weights and indicators, and enduring the ever-present tangles, I climbed out of the river and walked through the wind to the truck. I had fished for four hours and only got two fish to the net, but that last one made for a very memorable day.

Frugal Spaz

Cold, snowy weather and an out-of-town trip to visit family prevented us from visiting Chaffee County for four weeks, and on the fifth weekend Kathy had a commitment. But I was anxious to bring the truck back to Denver for the season and there looked to be a short break in the weather that would allow for dry mountain roads. So I suggested to Todd that maybe we could get some fishing in, and perhaps he could drive up so I could drive the truck back. At 2:30 Saturday afternoon – just a few days before Thanksgiving - Todd pulled up to my Denver house for the two-hour drive. The roads were indeed dry but the wind was unbelievable. I'm pretty sure I saw chunks of Utah blowing past the windshield. We pulled in at 4:30 just as it was getting dark and drove straight to a restaurant. Todd picked up the tab to show his thanks for inviting him up to fish. Over dinner and a beer we discussed, among other things, the merits of buying a bottle of craft whiskey at the local distillery to give my brother Dave for his birthday.

But at the distillery after dinner I was reluctant to fork over what was a fair chunk of cash for a smallish bottle. Plus I kind of wanted some for myself, but I am definitely too cheap to buy two bottles of craft whiskey. So Todd and I came up with a plan: along with a bottle, we would buy a stainless-steel flask engraved with the distillery's logo, fill it with whiskey and give it to Dave for his birthday. Todd and I would split the cost and whatever whiskey was left over. But when it came time to open my wallet, I tried to bargain with the bartender.

"What do the local liquor stores charge for this?" I inquired.

"I don't know, maybe a little less, like five cents," he responded ambiguously.

I was worried that if I went to the liquor store down the block they'd be selling it for $10 or $15 less. While I hemmed and hawed and acted reluctant in hopes of the bartender offering up some kind of deal, Todd got embarrassed by my cheapness, pulled out his credit card and made the purchase. This would not be the last time my frugality would embarrass Todd this weekend.

Once at the house we were greeted right at the front door by the unmistakable stench of a dead mouse. Todd opened the coat closet to discover a mouse in a trap, and tossed the mouse and trap onto the back steps to await disposal by the light of morning. After we got settled in a little, that shiny, new bottle of amber liquid tantalized us from the kitchen counter. So we buckled to the temptation and opened the whiskey, and then did ourselves a disservice by pouring it over crusty, off-smelling, five-week-old ice. We still enjoyed sipping it as we sat at the kitchen table rigging up our fly rods for tomorrow, using a new-to-us knot called the non-slip mono loop for tying on our nymphs. I also paid Todd my half of the whiskey purchase.

The thermometer read 20 degrees at first light and a stiff wind blew. When Todd got up an hour later we decided to go get breakfast. I opened up the coat closet to retrieve my jacket and was met once again with the overwhelming dead-mouse odor. The lingering morning cobwebs in my brain were instantly eradicated by the sudden, putrid blast.

Once at the restaurant I offered to buy breakfast. This is where my thriftiness once again embarrassed Todd. I have not always been cheap - well not *as* cheap - but a recent experience awakened some kind of primal instinct to save money. While out of town, Kathy and I were invited to go to a movie with our hosts. This was the first movie I had been to in 11 years, not because of my cheapness – I don't think – but because I just prefer to watch movies in the comfort of my own home. But at 56 years old, I discovered that I was eligible for the senior discount at this particular theatre. I still had to pay $200 for a small popcorn though, like everyone else. (If you are reading this in the future, say in five years when popcorn really is $200, then change the $200 to Eighty Billion dollars. That way you can tell I was being satirical. By the way, how's that flying-everywhere-in-your-office-chair thing working out? (Note to self: invent the Heli-chair (Chair-copter?) and make enough money to buy a popcorn in the future.)) But hey, if the movie theatre can offer me $3 off the price of a movie ticket without blinking an eye, maybe it's easy to save money just by asking. What a concept!

When I opened the menu the early-bird special jumped out at me: $5 between 6 and 8 a.m. for a choice of several breakfasts, including coffee. I looked at my watch: 8:05.

"What time did we sit down?" I asked Todd.

He looked at his watch and said, "I don't know, maybe eight?"

Just then the waitress walked up and put her hand on my shoulder. "Can we get the early-bird special?" I asked.

She looked at the clock on the wall and said, "Sure." I saw her kind of sniffing the air and then quickly take her hand off my shoulder. Now I smelled it too – my jacket, which I was still wearing, had absorbed the rancid-mouse aroma while in the closet.

I proceeded to order a $5 breakfast, as did Todd, and I ordered a side of bacon to share. When she brought our meals she said something about the bacon order being kind of skimpy, and to let her know if we wanted more. We quickly ate the bacon and when the waitress checked back after a bit I said, "Did you offer us more bacon?"

"I sure did, Hon," she smiled. Why do waitresses call everyone Hon? It must be one of the first things you learn as a server. "Call everyone 'Hon' Mabel, and touch their shoulder or arm, and your tips will be 31% higher." Anyway, she brought more bacon. (It is a known fact that 99% of all waitresses are named Mabel.)

Our two $5 breakfasts, plus the bacon and tax, came to $13.94. So I pulled out my frequent-diner card, which had been fully punched the last time here and made me eligible for a major discount of $10. This immediately indicated to everyone in the place that I was a big spender, worthy of special attention and praise. But alas it was not forthcoming. I reflexively reached for my credit card as Todd cringed. "Don't pay with a credit card for four bucks," he admonished.

"Huh?" I looked up to see him turning red. "Am I embarrassing you Todd?"

"Yes, now just put down some cash and let's go."

By now the waitress, alerted by our serious discussion over a $4 tab, stopped at our table and said sweetly, "Is everything OK, Hon?"

"Yes. Can you get us started on a new punch card?" I inquired. Out of the corner of my eye I could see Todd try to melt into the booth with embarrassment.

"I'm sorry Hon, you have to spend $10 to get a punch."

"Do you want to punch me in the arm?" I asked by way of apology.

"If it'll make you feel better," she said.

"I will," said Todd, "and it will make me feel just about right."

The waitress walked away shaking her head and I put $7 cash on the table, tipping $4 on the pre-punch-card total of $13.94, a tip that amounted to almost 30%. As we stood up to leave, thoroughly embarrassed Todd reached for his wallet and put down another $1.

After breakfast Todd drove the eight miles upriver to check on his winterized house and empty his mouse traps. I think he was also anxious to get away from me and my newly cheap ways. I got a few things done around the house, like setting up the heater at the well-head for the winter and cleaning up after the trap-caught mouse. I felt a little better about that single mouse when Todd returned and said his traps caught six mice.

We decided to fish a spot where Todd had some recent success, the Fisherman's Bridge area. The river is wide here as it flows through a flat section of the valley that is devoid of big trees – just head-high willow bushes lining the banks. We hoped we would benefit from the resulting sun on the water by landing numerous big trout. On a plateau above the east shore of the river is a gigantic dirt parking lot where rafters gather during the summer months for their adventures through Brown's Canyon. On the west shore are the buildings of a couple of commercial rafting enterprises that were closed for the season and eerily quiet. We parked along the road just beyond the bridge and picked our way down the embankment to the east side of the river. I had checked this area out a few years ago and decided that due to its flat appearance and lack of features I probably wouldn't have any luck here. And I was skeptical today as well, but Todd said he had caught several large fish here a few weeks ago, so I was willing to give it a whirl.

As usual, my initial casts were awkward until I got into the swing of things. Aw hell, all my casts are awkward - but even more so when I'm just starting off for the day. We both started with a Pat's Rubber Leg as an attractor pattern. I had a small Black Beauty below that, while Todd fished a Hare's Ear followed by a small nymph at the bottom of his three-fly rig. It was about 11:30, and the sun had warmed the air to around 40 degrees. The wind blew straight downstream, but had eased substantially from its earlier strength. We had been fishing for about an hour when I heard Todd whoop with excitement. I looked up to see that he had waded across to the west bank and had a fish on the line. Once in the net he held it up to show me a decent-sized brown trout.

"What did he take?" I yelled across the river over the sound of the rushing water.

"What?" Todd called back.

"WHICH FLY?"

"Hare's Ear."

"WHAT?"

"HARE'S...EAR!"

So I sat down on a rock along the shore to switch out my rig so it included a Hare's Ear. I fished that for a while, still without activity, before wading over to the west shore. That's when I realized how cold my feet were. At the first hint of seasonal cold water I wear two pairs of socks, with a foot-warmer packet stuck in-between. This has served me well over the last few years, but now these things must be beyond their effective date. I had bought them at a warehouse store in mass quantity; something like 60,000 of them came in a huge box. And my face was starting to feel raw from the wind blowing directly at us. And I wasn't catching fish - so the day was kind of sucking.

But once on the west side I sat down, right there on a rafting outfits "beach", and switched out my flies again, this time tying on a huge, heavy Golden Stonefly and a little red midge below that. I fished my way upstream for a few minutes, working a seam that separated faster and slower water, when I came to a mellow crosscurrent flowing into the main channel. *If I'm going to catch a fish today, this looks like the most likely spot.* My indicator subtly stalled in the current and I figured my bottom fly was just dragging the rocks, but I flicked my rod-tip upward anyway. *Hello!* A hearty tug greeted me in return. *OK, don't lose this fish, it will probably be your only chance today.* I made sure to keep the line taut and didn't try to net the fish before it was ready. After a few minutes I reached for the net to land the fish - my brand-new net that cost me a grand total of $1.45.

A discount, outdoor-product website had sent me a $20 coupon since I'm such a nice guy, and I found this supposed $40 net on their site for $20 during a free-shipping promotion. I had been using the net that belonged to a friend of Todd's after my giganto-net decided to escape downstream earlier in the year. But the friend was trying to sell his net for

$90 and I was afraid of losing that one too. So being the big-spender that I am, my after-tax total was $1.45 on the new net - and now was its first test. I put the net in the water, guided the fish toward it and landed the fish – on top of the net! The cheap-ass netting didn't accordion down and open up, so the fish was just lying there on top of the net. I gave the net a shake to try to get the fish down into the bottom, but instead I almost bounced it right off. So I quickly put my rod between my teeth so I would have a hand to grab the bottom of the netting from the outside and pull down on it. Luckily the fish cooperated during all this and soon found itself at the bottom of my stupidly stiff net. I don't know if the net is stiff because it's new, or because of the cold water (hopefully not!) or because it's a cheap piece of crap (more likely).

Surprisingly, the fish had taken the massive Golden Stonefly I was using as an attractor. By the time I had removed the fly Todd was there, camera in hand. "Just in time," I mumbled through the rod in my mouth.

"I came downstream when I saw you set the hook," he replied.

Todd took a few photos as I proudly held the 14-inch brownie, which was indeed my only fish of the day. When I looked at the photos later I saw that I still held the rod in my teeth. *What a spaz.*

Initially this is where this two-year story ended. But it was pointed out to me that the conclusion was a little abrupt and not warm and fuzzy enough. So in my best John-Boy Walton narration voice: After this weekend the weather returned to what you might expect from a Rocky Mountain winter. I would not fish again for three months, deciding against freezing my ass off by standing in an icy river, nymphing for lethargic fish in the bitter wind. But eventually the snows would melt and the winds would mellow, the sun would regain its strength, the water would warm and the trout would return to being more trout-like. And I'd be back in the river, trying to overcome my natural spazziness long enough to catch a fish or two.

Please enjoy this excerpt from the upcoming *Obtuse Angler - Volume 3.*

If Chris Farley Did a Doublemint Gum Commercial

Kathy and I decided it was about time we took a hike since our last one had been two months ago in Glacier National Park. After looking through our guidebooks and checking the map, we elected to hike to Waterdog Lake. A 40-minute drive put us at the 10,313 ft. trailhead, just 3 road miles and 1000 vertical feet below the summit of Monarch Pass and the Continental Divide. This was a short trail - 1.3 miles to the lake, but it was rather steep – gaining 1,077 ft. in elevation along the way. Our frequent, gasping-for-air stops were a rude reminder that we had not been hiking enough lately. It was also obvious that hiking above 10,000 ft. is considerably more taxing than hiking at 3,500 feet as we had done at Glacier. The result was that we travelled less than 1 mile per hour, taking 90 minutes to climb the 1.3 miles.

The trail was rocky and not particularly scenic, following power lines while rising through a mostly viewless pine forest. But the trail eventually veered away from the lines and once we reached the lake we forgave those who planned and built the trail, thankful that they had provided an opportunity for us to be at such a beautiful place. Kathy immediately reached for her camera and began photographing the small alpine lake reflecting the pine-covered hillsides, the nearby bald peaks and the white, cotton-candy clouds. I broke out the fly rod of course, but as usual the trees surrounding the lake were rudely interfering with my back cast. *Stupid trees.* The flies that I did get into the water, thanks to my shaky roll cast, were ignored by the actively feeding cutthroats that were crashing to the surface for something too small for me to see.

Eventually the nice, white clouds were driven away by mean gray clouds, which decided to have some fun and pelt us with hail. We accepted this invitation to leave, making it back to the truck in an hour – in which time the hail turned to rain and my rickety knees turned to mush. But as out-of-shape as I felt, I knew that there is always someone worse off. And we ran into him about halfway down the trail.

Three younger men – perhaps in their mid 30's – had stopped for a breather on their way up the trail. Each of them carried what looked to be 50 pounds of camping gear on their backs. Two guys - I'll call them Joe and John Gore-Tex – could have been twins. They were tall and dark-haired, had sparkling, white teeth and looked to be in good physical condition. I felt like I was watching an old Doublemint gum TV commercial with these guys and their brand-new, matching packs, sleeping bags, tent, pants, hats and rain jackets. The third guy, who I'll call Chris Farley for his amazing resemblance to the late, large, comedic actor, looked as out of place with these guys as, well, Chris Farley in a Doublemint gum commercial. He was considerably unkempt as he stood panting jacketless in the rain, his white cotton T-shirt sporting what looked to be several fresh chili-dog stains where it stretched to the breaking point over his prominent belly.

After we exchanged greetings, Farley asked us how much further it was to the lake, while at the same time trying to reach behind him without much success to secure loose gear that was ready to escape from his sweat-stained backpack. I was expecting his awkward gyrations to result in a slip in the mud and a tumble down the mountainside at any moment.

"About three quarters of a mile," I answered.

"Is the trail like this the whole way, or does it level off?" he asked.

I hated to say it but I did. "It gets steeper."

Farley looked crestfallen, standing there in the rain with his stained T-shirt, disheveled backpack and mop of wet, blond hair plastered against the side of his head. It turns out the three of them were planning to camp at Waterdog Lake that evening and in the morning, if Farley had survived, continue up to another nearby lake for a total of three days camping and fishing at altitude. As we bade them farewell and continued our way down the trail Kathy whispered to me, "That guy looks like a heart attack waiting to happen."

I responded, "He's probably saying the same thing about me right now."

Made in the USA
Lexington, KY
31 March 2018